LEITH'S GUIDE TO

SETTING UP AND RUNNING A RESTAURANT

LEITH'S GUIDE TO SETTING UP AND RUNNING A RESTAURANT

MARTIN WOOD

MEREHURST
LONDON

Acknowledgements

I would like to thank the following people for their invaluable support, criticism, advice and assistance in preparing this book:
Edward Bunting, Tony Cator, Lesley Ellis, Gillian Hutcheon, Prue Leith, Marilyn Newman, Rod Palser, Neil Place, Pamela Vandyke Price, Ronald Sharkey, Dale Stearn, Caroline Waldergrave and Beth Wood.

Published 1990 by
Merehurst Limited, Ferry House, 51–57 Lacy Road, Putney, London
SW15 1PR.

ISBN 1-85391-124-0

Edited by Lesley Ellis
Designed by Bill Mason
Typeset by Medcalf Type Ltd, Launton, Bicester, Oxfordshire.
Printed by Butler and Tanner, Frome, Somerset.
Cover photograph:
Chewton Glen, New Milton, Hampshire.
© Anthony Blake

CONTENTS

Foreword

Prue Leith

There is no doubt in my mind of the qualities it takes to make a restaurateur. They are energy, enthusiasm, and nit-picking attention to detail. Of course, it helps to have a great front-of-house personality. But bonhomie doesn't underwrite profits in quite the same way as dogged care does.

Potential restaurateurs are everywhere. Martin Wood's restaurant management courses at Leith's School of Food and Wine are packed with would-be entrepreneurs: ex-army officers who fondly think that retirement is compatible with running a nice quiet country pub; actors who feel it would be a good thing to have a second string to their bow; accountants who believe there are pots of money in fast food . . . Not all of these make it. When fantasies of instant fame and glory are replaced by real knowledge of the life of a restaurateur, many sensibly drop out.

That is why I think this book is important. It does not pretend to have all the answers, but it does give insight into what you will need if the glamorous dream of a restaurant is not to become the nightmare of bankruptcy.

I had some idea, when I opened Leith's 22 years ago, that I'd spend my time swanning about in great clothes, receiving plaudits and giving away brandies to favoured customers. In fact I spent our opening night in the ladies loo, plunger in hand. Leith's was packed from day one, but we lost money steadily for the first six months. I didn't watch the books, I didn't watch the waste, and I knew nothing of staff 'fiddles'. I thought great food and a happy atmosphere was all that was needed.

Happily, I'm a fast learner. But I could have been saved a lot of sleepless nights if *Leith's Guide to Setting up and Running a Restaurant* had been my bedside reading at the time.

INTRODUCTION

Owning a restaurant can bring moments of sublime pleasure, years of satisfaction and periods of sheer terror and heartache. I gained my first experience of professional catering on the grand scale when I was a student at the Scottish Hotel School and working part-time as a waiter in a vast, gilded ballroom in Glasgow's city centre. Running about that great room weighed down with haggis and neeps, grandly offering suspect wines and forgettable food and silver-serving whisky-sodden Burns' Night revellers taught me more than I could ever learn about restaurants in the academic perfection of the hotel school.

I left the school armed with the unlikely title of Bachelor of Arts in Hotel Administration and plunged into the corporate depths of the leisure industry, but after a couple of years abandoned suit and briefcase and fled back to the world of restaurants. Since then I have worked as chef, barman, waiter, restaurant manager, owner and consultant. I have designed restaurants, taught classes, peeled carrots and scrubbed floors. . . . Nothing beats practical experience for helping you cope with the day-to-day complexities of life as a restaurateur.

Becoming a restaurant owner is enormous fun, a process which allows for a great deal of free creative thought, the thrill of buying for an establishment, and the satisfaction of seeing the completion of an idea which the public can appreciate and enjoy.

Being a restaurant owner is an altogether different story; one full of stress, hard work at unsociable hours, and people, both staff and customers, exhibiting the usual human frailty of unreliability.

But ultimately, the constant combination of being creative, satisfying the public and coping with the daily unexpected, brings the reward of contented customers and money in the bank, and there are plenty of examples in the restaurant game where owners are happy, busy and enjoying their chosen profession.

This book attempts to steer the would-be restaurant owner through the maze of starting a business, and outlines ways of running a restaurant without the usual problems which, if unchecked, can lead to failure. The information is based on experience gained in opening and running over a dozen operations in the USA and the UK, and from lectures given in London and New York.

The philosophy of the book is based on the premise that the restaurateur is a caring person who respects the art and science of cooking and who respects and appreciates people who eat out in public. If the current vogue for tyrannical owner-chefs who bray and physically assault their media-created public appeals to you, then read no further. This book is for those who want to be professionals in their chosen path; a way of life involved with 'bonhommie', care and attention to every detail.

There are always certain people throughout a working life who inspire and provide a set of standards or a level of style, or who simply become heroes. Charles Chevillot (La Petite Ferme, New York), Donald Bruce White (caterer, New York 1970–1980), and Prue Leith (Leith's Restaurant, School, and Catering in London) are the top three on my list. They have individually provided me with inspiration, style, and a sense of professionalism.

NOTE

For ease of reading, I have used 'he', 'his' and 'him' throughout the book, and I trust this won't cause misunderstanding. It scarcely needs saying that both sexes are represented at all levels of the restaurant industry.

CHAPTER ONE

PLANNING THE BUSINESS

One of the many reasons why so many restaurants fail is poor planning. The elaborate new restaurant, designed to look expensive but where the menu is considered last of all, is a recipe for failure.

The concept for a restaurant must begin with the menu — from there the planning can begin. How much equipment is needed, and what kind, depends on the style of food and drink. The price of the menu denotes the style of the restaurant. The length and the variety of the dishes denote how many and what type of staff are required. The menu gives the customer an immediate idea of what sort of experience is likely to follow. And the menu displayed outside does exactly the same job as a shop window; it provides the passing customer with a sense of what to expect and how much it will cost.

After working out the price of an imaginary menu, some work is required to figure out the type of customer who will go for that menu, and hence where to locate the restaurant to sell it. Does the menu work for a lunch-time operation or evening? Can the restaurant provide a lunch service and dinner, and make money? All the relevant questions can be directly answered by producing a menu. The location, price, staffing, equipment and size can all be planned once the menu is established.

Each time I have been asked to work on a new restaurant, my first question to the owner has concerned the menu. Usually the answer has been negative, the menu being the last thing he plans to think about. Many restaurants have opened simply because an entrepreneur saw a site, believed that restaurants were easy places to make fast money, and instructed a designer and a builder to make a restaurant. The chef, the menu and all that sort of thing could wait until the place was built.

The first thing to do when starting a restaurant is to produce a menu. The only way to describe the concept is through the menu which is simply a list of your products, how they are prepared, and what they cost. To produce a menu a chef is required, and an accountant to check the costings. That is the first step.

MENU PLANNING

Write and cost a menu which reflects the food you choose to sell. The menu written at the early stages of planning will not necessarily be the eventual menu used on the first day of operation. It is simply a device whereby the tone, the style and the kind of food is indicated. It gives the planner an idea of the sort of equipment to install. Is a bar required, what sort of service is relevant to the menu content, and how is that service supported by staff and equipment? What utensils are needed and what sort of coffee will be served? Every detail on the menu has a message for the restaurant planner, and by producing a menu first, the restaurant owner has an immediate idea of what is involved in costing out the budget and working out a feasibility study to check if the project will be financially successful.

Menus are personal expressions of the taste of the restaurant owner who may or may not necessarily be a chef or waiter. The menu is a commercial document and must appeal to the market that is being catered for.

The first menu should contain everything, food, drink and service, that is available in the restaurant. Bread, butter, salads, tea and coffee, mineral waters, bar items,

SOME CONSIDERATIONS FOR MENU PLANNING

1. A balance of variety, with dishes which will appeal to a sufficiently broad spectrum of tastes.
2. A balance of texture, colour, and types of cooking.
3. An awareness of nutrition, the science of cooking, and an appreciation of the serious trends in healthy eating.
4. Knowledge of availability, seasons, and price fluctuations at the markets.
5. Originality: the ability to produce something new with familiar materials using different combinations of ingredients or seasonings, a change in service or presentation, or working with unusual items.
6. Size: of the menu, of portions, and of serving ware. What space is available in the kitchen; how many staff are required to service the menu; and what size should the portions be to fit within the expected price range?
7. Capability: the level of expertise available, the complexity of the cooking, the availability and cost of staff.
8. What is physically possible in the space and time allowed for cooking. Make sure there is a balance of pre-prepared and cooked-to-order dishes. Make sure that there are not too many grills for the chef to manage, or too many soufflés and roasts for the oven capacity.

wines, cigarettes, bar snacks, chocolates — everything that is bought and resold should be in the first menu along with a list of support services and products.

Having decided the structure of the menu, the interesting part begins — composing the menu itself. The decision taken by the owner, manager and chef at this stage will focus on the food that is going to represent the restaurant. It will be a combination of market requirements and the personal taste of the owner or chef. Every restaurant ultimately is known for the strengths of certain dishes. Only a handful with vast budgets can attain the heights of all-round culinary expertise.

Draft Menu Proposal for a New Restaurant

Lunch and dinner: 50 covers

Crudités and 1 hot canapé per session at the bar

Lunch

3 appetisers

4 main courses

3 desserts

Dinner

5 appetisers

6 main courses

4 desserts

Cheeseboard

Fruit basket

Garden salad

Coffee: house blend, espresso, decaffeinated (all freshly ground)
Teas: Lapsang, Keemun, Orange Pekoe

Sugar-dipped fruits and champagne truffles presented with bill
Selection of 6 brands of cigar

Liqueurs/ports/brandies

Full bar service

Wine list: 4 house wines, 1 Champagne, selection of 30 assorted wines
Mineral waters, fresh fruit and vegetable juices

When starting for the first time in the commercial world of selling food, a menu should be limited to the abilities of a fledgling kitchen and its crew. It is all very well to have a menu which is constantly changing, but the effort required to gear up to a completely new menu is tremendous and takes much experience on the part of the whole restaurant. So, make changes seasonally but within the range of familiar dishes, introducing new ones when the repertoire is thoroughly known. It is surprising how quickly a constant team can adapt and learn. The problems in developing kitchen expertise derive from an ever-changing succession of chefs and assistants.

Restaurants become successful by producing well-cooked food consistently. Press reviewers will recommend certain dishes, and the public who return expect the same standards. The development of regular business depends on this consistency from the kitchen.

Especially important in the early days of a business is the ability to offer first-class products, expertly served. No business should open its doors to the buying public without being familiar with every facet of the production and service. Only by starting with a simple menu can the beginner achieve this.

Eventually the menu emerges after discussion, tasting, restaurant-visiting, and argument. A menu is composed through consultation, and the chef's contribution is paramount. The menu is a commercial element of the marketing mix. Does it set trends or follow the existing ones? Does it educate, inform, and provide choices to cover a wide variety of tastes? Is it the expression of one person, the owner, who has no culinary background but knows what he likes? And who has the final say, owner, chef, consultant or restaurant manager?

Money can be made with operations which copy a well established format or with original concepts. The owner has the final say, the choices being made with marketing expertise, originality, and adaptation to prevailing conditions and experience.

Whatever the menu is for the opening day, it will surely be different in content and style from the menu which

A Sample Menu for Costing

50 covers: modern English/Continental cooking

LUNCH

Marinated wild salmon; dill and mustard sauce
Ravioli filled with spinach and ricotta in a cream sauce flavoured with oregano and garlic
Leek and Parma ham tart
Tomato, carrot and orange soup served with cheese straws

Haddock and smoked salmon fishcakes; parsley sauce
Steamed fillet of sole; beurre blanc
Grilled calf's liver with avocado, bacon and shallots
Poached chicken 'Aioli'
Chef's speciality of the season
Selection of seasonal organic vegetables

Fresh fruit tarts
Apple fritters and vanilla custard
Lemon cheesecake
Chocolate Marquise

Cheeseboard/fruit basket

Selection of freshly brewed leaf teas: Lapsang, Keemun, Darjeeling, jasmine

Selection of freshly ground coffees: house blend served in cafetières, Italian espresso, cappuccino, decaffeinated filter coffee, Columbian

Mineral waters: Evian, Malvern, Badoit, Apollinaris
Freshly squeezed organic vegetable and fruit juices

finally emerges to contain the standards and the idiosyncracies of a popular place with a regular crowd.

The finished menu needs to be produced early in the pre-planning stage. Apart from being a source of

DINNER

Scallop mousse; saffron and lobster sauce
Game terrine
King prawns marinated in ginger, soy and coriander
Artichoke and leek pie; lemon butter sauce
Trolley of hors d'oeuvres

Sea bass en croûte with fennel stuffing; fresh tomato sauce
Steamed salmon; mustard and caper sauce
Roast rack of lamb with provençale herbs and garlic; hollandaise sauce
Grilled duck breast with almonds; sage and orange gravy
Escalopes of veal with wild mushroom sauce
Chef's speciality of the season
Selection of seasonal organic vegetables

Hazlenut meringue and coffee layer cake
Steamed lemon sponge; raspberry sauce
Chocolate and mocha roulade
Canteloup sorbet

Cheeseboard/fruit basket

Selection of teas and coffees, mineral waters and fresh vegetable and fruit juices as above.

information for the designer and planners, it is required to provide a costing for the feasibility study.

THE FEASIBILITY STUDY

The feasibility study is the projection of the business cost and income and a forecast of profit or loss. Preparing such a projection requires an accountant or an experienced restaurateur, a chef, food and drink suppliers for information on prices, and market research.

Figures can show a business in any state depending on

the input. The chief purpose of preparing the projection is to show it to an investor or lender, which means it will be examined by financially experienced people. The best approach is the honest one, verging on pessimism. It is best to show a loss when losses usually occur, and to illustrate the requirements for operating capital calculated over a period of not less than two years, preferably over three.

The first step in preparing the projection is to calculate the size or capacity, the menu cost, and the frequency of serving meals over a weekly basis. Location is the other starting point. But which comes first — planning and costing a typical menu, or finding the right location for the business?

As soon as the idea of starting a restaurant becomes serious, the search for the location begins. But it is not necessary for the initial projection. A fair figure can be reached by working with the minimum number of seats required. However, the cost of space is an essential factor for the finished proposal and this can vary tremendously. So, prepare an initial projection based on the estimated desired capacity, and use a restaurant broker to give an indication of current market prices for leases and freeholds.

To discover the capacity from a given location, first calculate how much space diners take up in a restaurant. This will vary according to table size and shape and the type of seating used.

Usually the type of operation determines the space allotted to each diner. Fast food operations with a lower average spend require a high turnover; higher prices allow more space. A useful average of 1.4 sq m (15 sq ft) can be incorporated into the initial set of figures. This allows corridor space of 900 mm (3 ft) and chair access of 450 mm (1¼ ft).

How much of the space is divided between serving areas

and production? Again the type of operation determines this, but a rough indication would be one-third of the space devoted to production and two-thirds to service, including facilities such as the cloakroom area and pay telephone.

For more details on kitchen and dining room layouts, see Chapter 3, ***Restaurant Design****.*

THE COSTING EXERCISE

After calculating the capacity, the next step is costing and pricing the menu. This part of the feasibility study requires knowledge of current prices for food and drink. The key to profitability in the kitchen is the ability to purchase at the best price (*see page 63* ***Purchasing***).

For this exercise, the best approach is to contact wholesale suppliers and ask for price lists, or get quotes over the telephone. Spot suppliers who deliver in the area to other restaurants, check in the trade magazines, use reference materials such as *Yellow Pages*, *English Food Finds* (Henrietta Green) and the *Caterer and Hotelkeeper* information service (*see page 148* ***Suggested Reading*** *and page 145* ***Directory***).

The chef is needed at this point to determine recipes and ingredients for the dishes: everything required to make a dish, garnished and ready to serve, needs to be identified and costed, based on commercial methods.

Having established the cost for a given number of portions, find the unit cost and then apply the industry average gross profit percentage. This is the proportion of the selling price, after allowing for deduction of Value Added Tax (VAT), that is profit after the actual cost is deducted. All prices that are published must include VAT.

Cost operations aim to achieve a gross profit percentage of 60 per cent, with the cost factor therefore being the remaining 40 per cent. Size and quality determine the

AN EXAMPLE OF MENU COSTING

Leek and Parma tart: 10-in quiche tin — 4 portions with watercress garnish.

A shortcrust pastry case filled with chopped leeks, Parma ham, egg yolks, cream, seasoning, and topped with grated Parmesan cheese.

PASTRY

Ingredients	*Cost*
½ lb butter	60p
1 lb plain flour	15p
pinch salt	1p
water	

FILLING

Ingredients	*Cost*
1 lb leeks	28p
2 oz Parma ham	50p
2 shallots + 1 clove garlic	2p
1 pt single cream	55p
6 eggs	30p
Parmesan cheese	10p
garnish	5p
TOTAL COST:	£2.56p

amount of gross profit (GP). Generally, the larger and more expensive restaurants aim for a higher GP, perhaps 65 per cent or more, to cover higher overhead costs. Another point to consider when setting the GP is the market and the price the competition is asking for equivalent products and settings.

At this stage of pricing, an average must be used and one which is pessimistic will be more accurate. Only after some experience in buying, correct portion controls, and getting the menu right, can the new restaurant expect to achieve a realistic and constant level of gross profit. The amount of waste, for example, will have a serious impact on the gross profit/food cost percentages in the early days. Try a cost factor of 40 per cent for the feasibility study. This will illustrate to the potential backer or lender that the presentation is taking a realistic approach.

Some dishes will be very cheap to produce, others will have one high cost element, and it is sensible to try and bring prices into one category by rounding up or down.

The loss-leader concept applies to the restaurant menu as it does to many other retail operations, where a high-cost item has a lower mark-up to make the sale and to keep the prices within certain parameters. Fillet steak comes to mind or caviar, items which are popular but have a cost completely out of the normal range.

The amount of labour involved must be considered when pricing; the time taken for a complicated dish with pastry, a filling and a sauce, when compared with that of a piece of grilled fish, establishes the eventual mark-up.

Before the figure of net profit is calculated the cost of overheads is deducted from the gross profit. A list of the overheads in restaurant operations is given in *figure* 6 with the largest portion ascribed to wages and rent or mortgage. The overheads of any business are the costs of operating after the product has been accounted for. Industry averages show that wages represent 25 to 30 per cent of the gross turnover, or income, and the additional running costs represent a further 20 per cent, leaving an average net profit of between 10 and 15 per cent.

Finally, the loan repayment, interest and tax are deducted.

With any projection there is inevitably a great deal of guesswork based on the scant information available. Wages can vary tremendously, and the amount paid to the proprietor and partners can be a key factor. The amount of money borrowed and the interest payments are other areas where there will be guesswork. Remember that interest rates can double in a few years.

Fig 1

SALES FORECAST FOR A 50-SEATER OPERATION

FOOD AND WINE SALES
(including VAT)

SUMMER

Typical week	Lunch	Dinner
Average spend	£15	£22
Monday	10	12
Tuesday	10	12
Wednesday	10	15
Thursday	15	20
Friday	15	30
Saturday	20	40
Total income	1,200	2,838

WINTER

Typical week	Lunch	Dinner
Average spend	£15	£22
Monday	10	15
Tuesday	10	15
Wednesday	15	20
Thursday	15	25
Friday	15	35
Saturday	25	45
Total income	1,350	3,410

ANNUAL INCOME

Summer	25 weeks @ £4,038 =	£100,950
Winter	25 weeks @ £4,760 =	£119,000
		£219,950

INCOME PROJECTION

The average spend includes the average meal price plus the average liquor spend, net of service and VAT, with the same percentage mark-up for liquor as for food. (In operating terms this can be higher, say 25 per cent to 30 per cent as a liquor cost factor, depending on the overhead costs and the style of operation.)

To achieve a GP of 60 per cent multiply the cost by 2.5
To achieve a GP of 65 per cent multiply the cost by 3
For a GP of 70 per cent multiply by 3.3

Liquor sales on average account for one-third of turnover.

The frequency of operation has to be established at this stage for an accurate projection. In *figure 1* the restaurant is open for six days a week for lunch and dinner, closed on Sunday, and operates for 50 weeks of the year.

Remember to account for seasonal variations in making projections. If buying an existing operation there may be figures available, but approach them with caution. Market research is essential to try to discover the amount of business in comparable establishments in the area.

FORECASTING CASH FLOW

How is the calculation for the wage factor arrived at? In the example given in *figure 2*, with 50 covers there is provision for five full-time and two part-time staff, making a total wage bill of £7,200 per quarter or £550 per week. This figure does not include management drawings, and assumes a distribution of 10 per-cent service charge to front-of-house staff.

By plotting the flow of cash on a monthly or quarterly basis the lender can see when and how much operating capital is required. Additionally, there has to be an allowance for the worst possible case and ensurance that

Fig 2

CASH FLOW FORECAST FOR A MODEL RESTAURANT

50 COVERS
STAFFING: 5 FULL-TIME, 2 PART-TIME
PURCHASES at 45% of sales

Quarters	1	2	3	4	Total
Sales	45,000	50,000	55,000	60,000	210,000
Purchases	20,000	22,500	25,000	27,500	95,000
Wages	7,200	7,200	8,000	8,000	30,400
Rent & rates	6,250	6,250	6,250	6,250	25,000
Overheads	4,000	4,000	4,000	4,000	16,000
Capital expenditure	10,000	—	—	—	10,000
Miscellaneous	3,000	—	—	—	3,000
Value Added Tax	—	5,800	6.500	7,000	19,300
	50,450	45,750	49,750	52,750	198,700
Surplus/(deficit)	(5,450)	4.250	5.250	7,250	11.300
Closing balance	(5,450)	(1,200)	4.050	11,300	11,300

Break-even requirement for a 50-seat restaurant open 5 days per week:

Overheads as above	198,700
Less VAT	19,300
	179,400

Assuming average of £20 per head, income would produce after VAT: £17.40.

Therefore, number of covers required = £179,400 ÷ £17.40 = 10,310.

A 50-week year = 206 covers per week.

A 5-day week = 41 covers per day.

there is enough money available to meet all the expenses of operating for a certain period of time at the beginning. Three months would be a minimum, and happily for some there is no need at all to use this provision.

CAPITAL COSTS

For any projection to have full meaning, the capital cost has to be established.

Capital costs include:

- **Price of property or leasehold, and improvements.**
- **Deposits, legal and accountancy fees, permits, business rates.**
- **Insurance for building, contents and employees, and public liability.**
- **Agents' fees, graphic design fees and printing charges.**
- **Furniture for dining room, bar, office.**
- **Opening stocks.**
- **Pre-opening labour.**
- **Recruitment.**
- **Opening party.**
- **Utensils, machinery, register, telephones, safe.**
- **Kitchen equipment and machinery.**
- **Installation charges.**
- **Uniforms, linen supplies, bathroom supplies, cleaning equipment and materials.**
- **Managerial expenses, travel and research costs.**
- **Marketing, including publicity costs.**

Costing the list of requirements for opening a restaurant for the first time will be a major effort involving locating suppliers and comparing prices, getting quotes and estimates and dealing with a variety of tradesmen, craftsmen and, sometimes, cowboys.

There should be a realistic approach to calculating the final capital sum. Purchasing second-hand equipment will make a great difference to the estimates for kitchen installations, for example, while there must be an allowance for pre-opening salaries which includes time for training new staff and the complete run-through of operations.

With the completion of the financial projection, a description of the business is added: the style; the staffing; the market and the menu; a plan of the site with a description of the layout and samples of colours and so forth; a description of management and experience; plans for expansion.

Finally, the presentation should look professional, typed with a serious, modern typeface, enclosed in a binder, and including some well-drawn, architect-style layouts and the graphic designer's logo. Bashing it out on a portable at home does not show a professional approach from the start. Much inexpensive help in putting together a good-looking document can be had from high street printers who employ designers working desk-top computer publishing programs. Many have full-colour laser photocopiers too.

LOCATION

For the completion of the feasibility study the location must be chosen and that is one of the most difficult tasks of setting up, mostly because the negotiations involve parties all interested in the same outcome — a good deal.

Looking for a suitable location starts with identifying the sort of area where the restaurant will thrive. Then, a thorough knowledge of the area is required. Visit other premises and retail establishments to get a sense of who is buying what. It is surely more difficult to open in an unknown area than in a location nearer home; the connections built up living in any community provide various useful contacts.

Fig 3

INITIAL PROPOSAL FOR NEW RESTAURANT

NAME: BEACH CAFE, Brompton Road, London SW3.

CONCEPT: an American-style cafe open from 10.00 am to midnight. Casual style with beach themes – Caribbean/Hawaii/California. Healthy food and full bar. Full on licence.

MENU SPECIALITIES: fresh pizzas; pasta; English breakfast; full vegetarian section with daily specialities; fish/game; organic produce; fresh fruit/vegetable juices; speciality breads; carrot cake/banana bread/blueberry muffins; pancakes; real milk shakes; real ice cream.

BEVERAGES: wine list featuring wines from California/Australia and South of France; draught beers and lagers; cocktails/blender drinks; espresso/cappuccino; decaffeinated coffee; fresh leaf teas; full bar.

SOURCES OF BUSINESS: local residential area;
seasonal tourist business;
existing customers at other local establishments;
public relations for additional business.

STAFFING: £800–£1,000 per week.

PURCHASING COSTS:* estimated at 45%.

RENTAL RATES: £20,000 per annum.

POTENTIAL INCOME PER DAY:

Average spend:
early – £5
middle – £10
late – £15

Seating capacity: 75
Bar capacity: 30–40
Opening hours: 10.00 am to midnight, 7 days a week.
Max potential for one sitting at each session for one day:

75 × 5 =	375
75 × 10 =	750
75 × 15 =	1,125
	2,250
Add bar income	250
Max potential per day:	£2,500

CAPITAL COSTS

Lease purchase, goodwill and fixtures	160,000
Improvements: architect/designer/builder/ decorator	20,000
Equipment	2,000
Pre-opening labour	3,000
Stocks	2,000
Fees/permits/deposits	1,000
Printing and graphic design	1,000
Staff hiring expenditure	2,000
Travel and publicity	2,000
Contingency	7,000
	£200,000
Investment funds available:	£160,000
Loan required:	£40,000

FORECAST

	Year 1	Year 2	Year 3
Weekly sales	4,000	6,000	9,000
Annual sales (50-week year)	200,000	300,000	450,000

Less

1 45% Purchases + 25% Labour + 20% Overheads
2 40% Purchases + 25% Labour + 20% Overheads
3 35% Purchases + 20% Labour + 20% Overheads

POTENTIAL NET PROFIT BEFORE TAX AND REPAYMENTS

	Year 1	Year 2	Year 3
1	20,000	30,000	45,000
2	25,000	45,000	67,500
3	50,000	75,000	112,500

LOAN REPAYMENTS (less current interest rates)

	Year 1	Year 2	Year 3
£40,000	10,000	15,000	15,000

DISTRIBUTION OF PROFIT

	Year 1	Year 2	Year 3
1	10,000	15,000	30,000
2	15,000	30,000	52,500
3	40,000	60,000	97,500

* Purchasing costs here are over-estimated to illustrate typical first-year operations while industry averages are about 40%.

Remember when considering a site that the location determines success or failure.

POINTS TO CONSIDER WHEN CHOOSING A RESTAURANT LOCATION

- **The immediate area surrounding the site: is it business, retail, tourist or residential? The source of potential customers: offices, cinema, theatre, museums, shops. The density of street traffic, and other restaurants or bars in the vicinity.**
- **Accessibility: by car and public transport; for parking and loading; by a rear exit.**
- **The age and style of building; its listing, if important. Scope for improvement: is there possibility of expansion; is there a cellar, a rear yard, storage space, floor space above?**
- **When is the area busy and when quiet during the week and during the year? Is there a season for the location? Are weekends busier or quieter? Is there evening traffic or solely daytime?**

It is a hard task to find a suitable site, and one which requires knowledge of the area and experience in recognising good restaurant locations. There are certain sites which are in wonderful areas and which repeatedly fail no matter what form of operation is started. And there are restaurants in impossible locations which make a fortune.

A popular misconception is that the best site is necessarily in a gastronomic desert. Actually, the best site may be sandwiched between two already successful restaurants. You will get their overflow, and the public regards the area as an eating-out district.

Whatever method you use to find a location, work with several agents. Inspect as many different styles of operation as possible to gather technical information, study layouts, and go through the exercise of negotiating for a property, even if you have no interest in it. The experience is invaluable.

EXISTING PREMISES OR CONVERSION?

The easiest way of starting is to use an existing operation which serves food. It could be a sandwich bar, a cafe, take-away or wine bar. It could require no change at all, or it could require a complete transformation.

The disadvantages include the possibility of a poor location with previous failures, prohibitive costs, a short lease, structural problems and the cost of goodwill.

The alternative is to convert a site. Installing a new restaurant can be easier and possibly cheaper than converting an existing one. The prospect of raw space, the advantage of planning from scratch, and the opportunity to create a different style could compensate for the officialdom, planning consent, and general hassle encountered when building a restaurant.

Conversion requires professionals: architect, kitchen installation experts, builder, plumber, electrician, Fire Officer, building regulations inspector, air-conditioning/extraction installers, bar builder. Each professional charges professional fees, except the kitchen installation experts who make money on the sale of equipment. Make sure they do not sell you more equipment than you need.

Does the advantage of a good location determine an increase in the budget? The risk of over-extending for the sake of a prime spot is one of the reasons that restaurants are known as high-risk investments. The capital required for opening is high, and the chance of success or failure is equally high. The right concept in a prime location can reduce some of the risk. But before taking on such a project, consider what finance and experience are available and what the market research indicates.

Certainly the logical way of starting is to take over an existing premises with the minimum of change and a low outlay of opening capital. The adventurous professional

CAPITAL EXPENDITURE FOR RESTAURANT AND BAR

Equipment, construction and administrative costs
Building and renovations
Construction materials
Construction labour
Plumbing
Electrical
Bar construction
Bar equipment
Lighting
External signing and graphics
Menu holder
Tables and chairs
Banquettes and bar seating
Floor covering
Music system
China, glass and silverware
Service equipment
Linen and uniforms
Ice machine
Kitchen equipment and utensils
Heating, air conditioning, extraction and fire-extinguishing system
Bathroom accessories
Cash register
Office equipment
Opening stocks, liquor and food
Maintenance equipment
Decor accessories
Printing: *stationery, menus, bookmatches, business cards, napkins, coasters, bill heads*
Licence fees
Architect and designer fees
Legal fees
Deposits: *telephone, utilities, rental equipment*
Rent deposit and security
Advertising and promotional expenses
Pre-opening labour
Opening party
Menu research costs
Accountant's fee
Insurance
Permits: *fire, health, business licence*
Rates
Operating capital
Contingency fund

from a catering background, with a following and financial backing, might opt for a new installation. The enthusiasm for such (ad)ventures can be infectious and the imagination and skills of a youthful, hard-working chef coupled with financially secure partners often produces interesting results.

Another choice when determining the location is whether to buy or rent. Again, the location itself is the main factor. Location is King; rent if you must, if it is for sale try to buy it.

Leasing is the usual way of getting into business. Few

city operations are for sale as freeholds. More so in rural areas. The problems with leases are their length and their rent increases. The shorter the lease, the less security there is for the restaurant and its borrowing power. A longer lease could be used as security against a loan, as well as providing a form of psychological security. Ownership of property adds another dimension to a business, providing attractive prospects to investors and lenders, and the freedom to alter without permission. The right to assign or sub-let is a major consideration before signing a lease. This problem doesn't occur in outright ownership.

Negotiating to buy a building can be more straightforward than arranging a satisfactory lease. With purchase, the negotiations rest on the price. With a lease there are several aspects: length of tenure; frequency of rent increases; rates, repairs and improvements; the right to assign or sub-let; and the initial rent payment structure.

A good lease for the restaurant proprietor would include a free start-up period, possibly three months; a low rent for the first year with escalations after year two, three and four; some incentive for the landlord to frequent the restaurant with credit or free meals; an option to buy the building; a sensible figure for goodwill and fixtures and fittings. However, signing a new lease means that the payment of rent is the responsibility of the original lessee — throughout the full term of the lease.

Remember that ultimately the deal rests between the restaurateur and landlord. If the location is right, the price within the realms of possibility and there is room for some compromise, then the only advice can come from intuition. Listen to an accountant and lawyer and anyone else with experience, and understand that restaurants are operations to be run as businesses requiring business-like management and enterprise; and the first decision to get hold of a property has to be a business decision.

It is worth trying to meet the landlord as soon as

possible for direct negotiations. Agents will always try to inject urgency, other interested parties being the classic ploy. With face-to-face meetings, the interests of both sides can be identified without too much use of the legal time normally involved in such deals, and will provide the opportunity to get to know the landlord and establish a working relationship. There is an advantage in persuading the landlord to approve of and have enthusiasm for the project.

In some cases there is no identifiable landlord, simply an organisation with a department for leasing its properties. In this situation a rent negotiator can be retained to strike a better deal.

Lease negotiations take patience and determination and a lawyer who acts quickly, preferably one with some experience of restaurants. If you have no personal experience of renting commercial premises, a lawyer will be essential. Engaging a lawyer who specialises in this particular aspect of the law can pay off, especially when dealing with a complicated licensing application.

Conversion may require planning permission from the local authority and permission for change of use of the premises. Some of the common problems that occur with conversions are the need for exhaust filter and duct work to clear residential accommodation, the need for secondary exits and fire-break facilities for neighbouring residential buildings; local concern about noise, rubbish and increased parking; signing, illumination, and obtaining liquor licences.

Regulations concerning fire, health and safety should be studied before looking at sites. Fire exits, load-bearing factors, access, power and water supplies, drainage and sewage lines, and environmental health requirements need checking after the first view of any site worth consideration.

There is no definition for the ideal restaurant location;

it either works or fails. Only with imagination can a restaurant be visualised where previously there may have been a carpet showroom, or a loft overlooking a cemetery at the back end of Fulham.

When I opened my first restaurant in New York I found a dowdy antique shop on Madison Avenue at a time when the property market was in the doldrums and leases could be had for $2,000 a month for a fifty-cover operation. For three days and nights I sat in that place, empty of all the stock and fittings and looked around examining the light, the proportions, the views. I absorbed the atmosphere; every building has one and every space has a feel all of its own.

I invited three or four close friends to come and sit with me and I outlined the plans I had in mind; the location of the bar, the kitchen, where the toilets would be. I showed them downstairs to the cellar, pointing out imaginary wine racks and the safe.

I spent hours watching the people walk by, looking at their clothes, noticing the shopping bags, overhearing conversations as I pretended to wait outside for someone late for an appointment.

I brought in a builder and then a restaurant equipment dealer with a string of bars, coffee shops and diners as a pedigree. He knew all the ins, outs, and sideways. And everyone agreed that it could work, that it was possible from all their points of view. But in the end, my reason for going ahead was my intuitive sense that the place was right for what I had in mind. It is that sense which provides the necessary kick-start to get on with a project with enthusiasm, not realising quite how difficult the problems will be. But the initial enthusiasm for a location should increase as the project becomes more of a reality. If it does not and that one-hundred-per-cent enthusiasm is fading, then stop.

CHAPTER TWO

RESTAURANT FINANCES

With the capital cost established, the search for money begins. Armed with the complete feasibility study and presentation, you approach the challenging process of persuading others to part with some cash.

The ideal situation for the restaurateur is to be sole owner, either using personal sources of finance or borrowing against assets such as a property or with a guarantee from a third party. Borrowing money is an expensive game and restaurants, being high-risk investments, are not popular with the larger banks and institutions, especially with no proven track record.

The alternatives lie in a partnership, or forming a company with a number of investors, or lenders, which is the case in the majority of small establishments. But the problem of mismatched personalities can arise in such associations. The ideal is for the restaurant owner/operator to have majority control with the partners or investors as minor shareholders. This requires a belief on the part of the shareholders in the special abilities of the operator. More often the first-time owner will have a minority interest as the only way of getting a project open.

Occasionally the operator will have no financial input, substituting talent for cash and linked by an employment agreement. This is usually the scenario for future breakups or worse. The fledgling chef or waiter with a good following elsewhere puts a deal together only to discover later that the investors have shifted their original intentions and begun to change the style, the staff, or simply to take it over.

A sincere investor will devise a suitable employment agreement giving some incentive to the operator without capital. The ability to purchase shares at certain specified periods, the freedom to set menus, hire and fire and establish policy, and the existence of a non-competing clause can be a form of protection for the investors, although hard to implement. Essentially, the would-be owner must put in some capital and show a willingness to risk money on the chosen project. It shows faith.

For partnerships to work the business must come first, allowing for the eventual clash of personalities and arguments long into the night. The difficulty lies in clashing egos and a struggle for control. The traditional flare-ups between kitchen and floor are nothing compared with the simmering resentment between business partners or an operator and his investors.

Too often an investor with no original intention of becoming a restaurant operator believes overnight that it can be done better and manoeuvres to gain overall control. The outcome is usually a messy divorce. Meaningful partnerships exist only when there is mutual respect for the strengths and weaknesses and when there are complementary personalities. Examine the relationships between partners when they are in equal charge, one in front and one at the stove. It can work provided there is an emotionally stable background and when the areas of responsibility are clearly defined.

As a business grows, partners change or circumstances may dictate a change of structure. Consider the possibility of unpredictable behaviour and chance occurrence, and make sure there is protection for personal investments and full participation, as well as the agreed split of assets and liabilities.

Whether the capital is borrowed from a bank or from

private sources, the lender primarily is looking for the ability of the business to survive while paying back the loan with the agreed interest. Naturally some form of security is needed, even for a limited liability company, but the most important aspect of the loan arrangement is the proof that the business has the right experienced personnel, a good location and a product that is likely to be popular in the chosen market.

When the business becomes operational, investors, lenders, partners and officialdom in the form of the Inland Revenue will need to see evidence of the financial state, trace the cash flow, note the expenses and marvel at the bottom line. Whatever the system of accounts, some careful study is required for the special requirements in restaurant accountancy practice. This subject is far too detailed to cover here, but *see page 148* ***Suggested Reading*** for recommended books on the subject.

If your accountant has no previous restaurant experience it might be worth finding a specialist for regular checks or to establish the correct control procedures at the beginning. It is an advantage to use an accountant who appreciates food and drink as well as the development of a sound relationship.

At the core of any system is the need to record cash and bank records, the cash book. This records weekly sales (restaurant; bars; tobacco; sundries) and other receipts, and weekly payments, including purchases and wages. The accountant needs this record to prepare the final summaries of the business, the trading accounts, and the balance sheet. The record of income and expenditure is made every week from the daily summary sheets or print outs, and it is this record which allows the management to track the costs of food, liquor and wages.

The accountant will also want a separate record of the following categories: Value Added Tax (VAT), tips, credit card sales, wages, purchases (food, drink, maintenance),

Fig 4

THE COLUMNAR CASH BOOK

CASH RECEIPTS

Date	Account to be credited	Reference	Sales				Total cash	Other receipts	Bank
			Restaurant	Bars	Tobacco	Sundries			

CASH PAYMENTS

Date	Account to be debited	Reference	Purchases				Wages	Other payments	Total cash	Bank
			Food	Drink	Tobacco	Sundries				

petty cash, operating costs (rent, rates, power, telephone, laundry . . .), capital costs (improvements and repairs), drawings for owners and investors.

With all the information on income and expenditure, complete with bank statements and cheque books, an accountant will be able to produce a monthly set of figures, giving a complete financial analysis of the business.

By breaking down the figures to show what each area of the business makes, along with percentages, the profit and loss sheet can be used as an analytical tool for management. It highlights the strengths and weaknesses of the restaurant and builds to provide comparisons for seasonal fluctuations.

Perhaps the chief reason for emphasising control procedures in the restaurant is to combat fraud. Personal vigilance and a control system provide the means but no system has yet been discovered which is completely fraudproof.

Some examples of fraudulent behaviour commonly found in restaurants include:

- **Collusion between kitchen and floor — issuing dishes without check exchange.**
- **Ripping up checks and pocketing the cash.**
- **Short-changing and overcharging.**
- **Stock brought in and sold for cash which is pocketed (especially liquor).**
- **Selling stock to other businesses (especially food).**
- **Writing up substitute bills and pocketing the difference.**
- **Outright theft.**
- **Use of stolen credit cards, running off more than one slip at each transaction.**
- **Suppliers adding the date into the total, short-weighting and overcharging.**

As restaurants grow in business and size, more controls are needed. A manual system to begin with helps to understand what sort of computerised method is best for your future expansion. Using serialised check pads and bills is the first step in setting up a control mechanism. And a regular marrying up of duplicate to original at the end of service indicates to staff that there is a form of control that will show up the basic fraud of ripping up the order. Some establishments will charge the waiter a fixed amount for a check missing from the sequence which cannot be accounted for.

Tracking the flow of money and working out regular costs of food and liquor manually will take a considerable amount of time. The other essentials of record keeping should be performed either by a regular bookkeeper or by computer.

The collection of VAT can be a sensitive area. The temptation to spend the government's cash has caused many a downfall. If you accept the simple fact that the restaurateur is an unpaid government tax collector, then VAT and all the clerical work entailed need not be a problem. Every day when the summary is done, the amount of VAT is calculated. The next day the money is banked and it is at this stage that the VAT is banked separately in an interest-bearing facility that allows easy withdrawals. Only in this way will VAT collection not provide false security. Pay it in and forget about it until the end of your VAT quarter.

As the business develops and there is more sophisticated knowledge about the business, the VAT money can be used creatively, providing there is sound financing and efficient bookkeeping.

Another time-consuming area is the payroll. Whatever policy is decided about casual or part-time staff and their method of reward, records must be kept. A name and address are basic essentials, a tax code number and

National Insurance (NI) details are also desirable. Beware of the temptation to pay unrecorded cash for labour, and realise what the penalties can mean. The fines imposed for income fraud are severe. Income tax also affects tip payouts and some establishments deduct the tax prior to distribution. This depends on whether the waiters declare their own earnings as self-employed, or receive their wages and tips net of taxes and NIS contributions. If there is no tip added to a bill then the waiters are presumed to declare what they receive, the house having no knowledge of the gratuity given. Remember, the restaurant owner is responsible for all income earned in the establishment, tips included. And tax inspectors can estimate tip earnings if no service charge is included.

Regular stocktaking, of liquor especially, provides the physical back-up to the weekly summaries and will show up any outstanding examples of shortages. Ultimately, the amount of bookkeeping performed in the restaurant and by the accountant can represent an expensive running cost. The installation of automated systems should always be contemplated from the start, but only by using a semi-manual system to begin with can the accounts procedures be understood fully and then, later, the advantage of computer-based systems can be thoroughly appreciated. Professional liquor auditors can be hired. They are expensive but may be worth their hire as deterrents as well as policemen.

A further advantage in establishing a good break-down of the figures, into lunch and dinner, food and liquor, is the use of analysis to determine popularity of certain dishes, amounts spent on appetisers, main courses and desserts, and discovering items with high gross profit margins. Remember 'the books' are a useful tool. Get to enjoy doing them. If they are pushed aside in favour of more exciting work, bankruptcy will follow.

The gifted restaurateur, creative in the kitchen and a

Fig 5

MANAGEMENT STATISTICS FOR A MODEL RESTAURANT

WEEKLY SALES REPORT

	LUNCH		DINNER	
	Sales	Covers	Sales	Covers
Monday	163	41	252	28
Tuesday	190	49	346	38
Wednesday	210	60	353	40
Thursday	186	64	240	24
Friday	173	62	884	92
Saturday	104	40	1327	140
All week	£1026	316	£3402	362
Average spend	£3.25		£9.40	

RANDOM MENU POPULARITY ANALYSIS

	No. of dishes	%
Starters		
Gazpacho	6	19
Crab cheese toast	3	9
Stuffed mushrooms	12	36
Avocado prawns	9	27
Melon	3	. 9
	33	100
Main Course		
Lasagne and salad	5	6
Chicken Kiev	22	25
Brochette of lamb	11	12
Dover sole	12	13
Sirloin steak	24	27
Fillet steak	15	17
	39	100

RANDOM POPULARITY ANALYSIS

	No. of dishes	%
Under £3.00	10	11
£3.00 to £5.00	16	18
£5.00 to £7.00	5	6
£7.00 to £8.00	38	43
£8.00 to £10.00	15	17
Over £10.00	5	5
	89	100

personality in the dining room, must also recognise the importance of providing the business with proficient bookkeeping. There is a particular talent in keeping a well organised set of books and each system is the reflection of the bookkeeper. The organised individual with a head for figures is not often found in the kitchen, more often out in front. If the creative genius in the equation is the owner, then there must be a financial partner or employee. The amount of work in restaurant accounts is essential and cannot be avoided.

Experience in the realms of restaurant finance brings the benefit of specialised information about various aspects of income and expense, the importance of estimating credit card discounts in a projection as one example. The amount of commission charged by the popular credit card organisations varies considerably and can be negotiated, the volume of sales is usually the main criterion and the frequency of cashing in the vouchers. A weekly payment of American Express (AMEX) vouchers will cost a half per-cent point more than if the payment was made monthly.

Does the establishment need credit card business? High-volume business at lunch-time with executive types demands the availability of credit card facilities. A lower-priced establishment encouraging faster turnover could have a cash only policy. The choice of cards, if any, can affect the income of a new restaurant by as much as five per cent of the credit card turnover.

The treatment of staff meal expenses is another example. In the restaurant business the majority of establishments regard staff meals as a labour cost and the cost of such food is either credited to the purchases account and debited to a staff meals account in the ledger, or adjusted in the trading or profit and loss accounts, where staff meals are shown as deducted from the purchases for resale. In either case the cost is shown in

Fig 6

END-OF-YEAR TRADING/PROFIT AND LOSS ACCOUNT FOR A MODEL RESTAURANT

	Amount	*Ratio*
SALES		
Food	99,592	60.0
Liquor	66,394	40.0
	165,986	100.0
COST OF SALES		
Food	45,759	45.9
Liquor	32,533	49.0
	78,292	47.2
GROSS PROFIT	87,694	52.8
DIRECT EXPENSES		
Wages and staff costs	33,326	20.1
China, glassware, cutlery and silver	580	.3
Linen hire	3,567	2.1
Cleaning and hygiene	942	.6
Flowers	830	.5
	39,245	23.6
ESTABLISHMENT EXPENSES		
Rent	8,521	5.1
Rates	2,445	1.5
Light and heat	2,913	1.8
Repairs and maintenance	236	.1
	14,115	8.5
ADMINISTRATION AND SELLING		
Advertising	1,783	1.1
Credit card charges	1,660	1.0
Insurance	240	.1
Motor expenses	1,663	1.0
Postage	506	.3
Printing and stationery	1,306	.8
Telephone	683	.4
Miscellaneous	586	.4
	8,427	5.1
FINANCIAL AND OTHER		
Accountancy	1,500	.9
Bank charges and interest	554	.4
Loan interest	1,400	.8
Depreciation	22,832	1.7
	6,286	3.8
	£19,621	11.8%

Fig 7

END-OF-YEAR BALANCE SHEET FOR A MODEL RESTAURANT

FIXED ASSETS		
Improvement ot leasehold premises		17,350
Fixtures and equipment		9,833
Furniture and soft furnishings		8,750
Motor vehicle		2,419
China, glassware, cutlery and silver		3,000
		41,352
CURRENT ASSETS		
Stocks	6,800	
Debtors and pre-paid	799	
Cash in hand	1,636	
	9,235	
CURRENT LIABILITIES		
Creditors and accruals	12,163	
Bank overdraft	6,176	
	18,339	
NET CURRENT LIABILITIES		(9,104)
NET ASSETS		£32,248
FINANCED BY:		
Proprietor's capital account		
Capital introduced	10,769	
Profit	19,621	
	30,390	
less Drawings	8,142	22,248
Business development loan		10,000
		£32,248

the profit and loss account as an expense.

The benefits of computerisation give the experienced restaurateur immediate information on the operation: the sales mix, the stock turnover, the sales per seat and per waiter, and current food and liquor cost percentages. But a well organised manual system planned with the minimum of sophistication can provide accurate records for summary and analysis. The biggest drawback to the manual system has to be illegible scrawl and arithmetical mistakes; these two factors alone can take up much time in re-checking.

At the end of the financial year (a date determined by tax considerations at the opening) two summaries have to be prepared. The first is a trading profit and loss account for the year. This will show the gross profit — the difference between the sale and the cost of goods sold — and the net profit which is the gross profit minus all other expenses. The second requirement is a statement of the company's financial position on the last date of the financial year — the balance sheet. This will summarise the assets owned and the debts owed, the difference being the capital value of the organisation as represented by the capital invested by the owner/investors and the profits retained in the business.

The undisciplined nature of many restaurant people has prevented many an accountant from providing accurate financial information. Any business which has such a mixture of cash and credit business with perishable and costly stocks to maintain has to install effective control mechanisms and proper records for a detailed breakdown of resources, income and expenditure.

Computerised systems nowadays provide the restaurateur with a cost effective way of reducing paperwork and combating fraud. However, it is worthwhile emphasizing here that the amount of clerical work in keeping records up-to-date and in such a way as to provide weekly analyses of costs, means that a budget must be set aside to cover the salary to provide the accountant with these details.

A successful accounting operation becomes so through the combination of creativity and discipline; it is up to the staff to make that combination effective and this relies on the quality of their input and accuracy. Without understanding the need for such controls as serialised checks, regular stocktaking, spot checks on portion sizes, staff will be uninterested. An effective system develops with participation, training, and incentives as rewards for adhering to the mechanical controls that have been established to guard the flow of money. Your profits are in the hands of your staff.

CHAPTER THREE

RESTAURANT DESIGN

Restaurant design is basically concerned with layout and decor, the allocation of space and the creation of a setting which enhances both food and customers.

The designer's brief derives from the menu; preparation and service of all the food and drink has to be achievable for a full restaurant — the first law in restaurant design.

Design the restaurant as if it were full. First, provide the right areas for the restaurant to function, to produce hot and cold food, to store and serve alcohol, to accommodate people and their belongings, to provide facilities for both staff and guests. Function comes first, the dressing is next.

For an idea of what is involved when laying out a restaurant, try the walk-through exercise: approach a restaurant; notice every detail, the sign, the light sources, the frontage, the door handle. Enter and notice the floor, the light switch, the exit sign. Make a list of items and their backgrounds and see where you would improve. Notice the things which stand out or jar. Watch how the staff flow between kitchen and dining room. Observe customers as they find the cloakroom or toilets, or use the telephone. What is the noise level, and why are the tables laid out in a particular way?

Many restaurants open without using a designer, professional or otherwise. But the proportions, the light, the architectural details, the size, the shape, all play a part in creating the atmosphere that presents itself to the prospective owner. A professional designer notices these details and endeavours to enhance the natural lines, the original shape and the lighting.

The natural behaviour of the customer is based on curiosity. Lifting a plate, feeling silk flowers in case they are real, viewing artwork; there is plenty of time for lazy or acute observation when sitting at the restaurant table. Everything comes under the closest scrutiny, and careless interior design results in visual indigestion. Good design takes care of details; an amateur attempt ignores them.

Every item should be chosen with the whole interior in mind. Integration and recurring themes ensure that the finishing touches to a room belong to the picture that is being created, bearing in mind the view from each chair. The purpose of design is to achieve an environment pleasing to the eye and easy on the palate, to create a memory of something pleasurable which touches all the senses.

The technique should be to allow the customer and the food to stand out with appropriate use of colour, texture and lighting. In any commercial operation, whatever the style of service, there is a need for professionalism at some stage in the planning and design. The interior represents the taste of the owner to the public, and the owner/designer must be objective and search out experienced advice if a professional is not engaged.

Sometimes the amateur approach can be charming. A typical 'I want to open a restaurant' story involves the couple who entertain well enough at home, decide to go commercial and open up an extension of their dining room; white walls with a hint of apricot, safe prints, some red somewhere, the odd piece of mahogany, Laura Ashley in the loo and a touch of Conran in the kitchen.

There is nothing wrong with any of the above; those designers have simplified, cleaned up and introduced brightness and colour into many previously drab and cluttered environments.

The temptation for the opposite extreme often inflicts the diner surrounded by modern restaurant design. The spaceship approach will always look dated, and art-for-art's-sake has encouraged many indulgences by frustrated home decor pro/ams who suddenly get their chance with a public showplace and romp away.

There is an opportunity with a restaurant to create an environment which would be rare to find in an average dining room. It is quite possible to create memories without the use of chrome tractor seats for barstools, yet there are several examples of great looking restaurants where black and white are the predominant colours.

One of the most important aspects of design is graphics. The first encounter with a restaurant is probably that of the sign with the name in a certain style or typeface. This, the logo or graphic representation of the restaurant's identity, indicates in letters, shapes and colour the style of the business. Of all the tasks involved in pulling together a restaurant, this is the one that must be handled professionally. Only a skilled graphic designer can translate the owner's vision, with the use of the menu and a sense of the interior, into a visual form.

NOTES ON PLANNING AND DESIGN

The exterior, entrance and hallway

Points to consider include whether there is enough space to enter comfortably, whether the entrance is for deliveries or if there is a rear access, and whether the door opens out or in. Can the customer be seen when entering the restaurant? What form of signing is there to indicate and advertise the restaurant? Will a menu be on display, and will it be visible from the street? Also, consider the seasonal requirements for the entrance and hallway: a cloakroom in winter, ventilation in summer, draft exclusion, or preferably a double-door lobby as even briefly opened doors in mid-winter make nearby tables uninhabitable.

The bar

This needs a gutsy approach, not an attempt to hide its real function. Bars in pubs have atmosphere when the message is drink and they feature the incidentals which contribute to that service. Beer pumps, ice bucket, illuminated bottles, bar equipment, the bits and pieces needed to make cocktails, soda syphons, shakers and swizzle sticks . . . all these are integral parts of the bar service and need displaying where they can be easily reached.

A properly constructed bar will be comfortable to sit or stand at, will have the correct rail for propping up a tired elbow and at the same time will look good. There must be enough space to work behind it, with everything at hand for efficient service.

The bar acts as the buffer zone between the door and the dining room and enables the bartender to control certain functions for the whole restaurant —cash, lighting, telephone and music, as well as all the beverages.

There must be adequate storage for cold drinks, wines, beers, and ice, and space for washing, drying and storing glasses. A cash register and a telephone need to be located at the bar, and there must be access to the reservation book, a system for storing and recording checks and bills, credit card facilities, and a place to keep menus. Fully operational bars need a cellar or additional space nearby for draught beers and bottle storage.

Without a bar, all these functions require a space somewhere in the restaurant, usually the kitchen. With a bar, there is the convenience of putting all the accompaniments to the meal in one place and increasing the amount of liquor sales through good display and ease of service.

Having a bar that looks like a place to enjoy a drink is a vital element of a substantial restaurant and should be enjoyed, by owner and customer. Of course there are restaurants, especially small country ones, or cafes that simply do not need bars.

The dining room

The choice and arrangement of tables and chairs is critical for successful flow and circulation. Factors to consider are style of service, speed of service, and average spend. The layout also takes into account the groupings of customers and this decision can seriously affect income. Adaptation is necessary in the dining room to cater for twos, threes, fours, and sixes. Whether choosing round or square tables, banquettes or chairs, the space determines the number of diners, and the choice of seating and table shape will affect that number, either comfortable and designed for a longish stay, or the opposite to achieve a high turnover with seats occupied for the shortest time.

Plans of the restaurant are needed for several purposes including licensing authorities, planning applications, and the builder. And by using a set of drawings, the designer can more accurately describe the plans, and change the layout with a set of movable scale models of tables and chairs. A simple way to start is to trace the layout on the floor with chalk, paper or string, but eventually plans and finished drawings will be needed.

Waiter stations are needed for storage in the dining room; the more items which can be stored out of the kitchen the better. A refrigerator, for example, may be incorporated into a waiter's station.

The location of the kitchen door can be a difficult choice. The flow is important here, even at the risk of losing a table. Sitting customers near the kitchen door (the 'Siberia syndrome') is asking for trouble, so avoid the problem.

Whether to incorporate the kitchen into the dining area comes down to a question of atmosphere. There can be something cheerful about the sights and sounds from a working kitchen and it certainly provides an incentive for cleanliness and order, while screens, double-hinged doors and non-fluorescent lighting can help to separate the two areas.

Track the main flow paths, from the kitchen to tables, and from bar to tables. Remember the need for cloakroom facilities, toilets and telephone and the access demands for these areas.

Chairs Most time in a restaurant is taken up sitting down. Hence the importance of choosing the appropriate chair. How much space will it occupy? Is it comfortable with arms and upholstery, or does it serve the minimum purpose uncomfortably? How much of the chair is seen when occupied, and how well does it score for noise, hygiene and longevity? While fixed seating such as banquettes takes up less space, the lack of flexibility can be a disadvantage, especially for large parties.

Tables Size is the important consideration, and the planning of table capacities must take account of legs or pedestal bases, height and adaptability. Round tops can be placed over squares, or flaps on hinges can increase the size. Larger round rings can also be used for adapting round tables. If cloth operations are used, then consider the need for some form of padding, to protect the surface from liquid spills and retaining odours.

A pedestal base provides solid support and takes up less space than legs; but legs can look better, especially when cloths are short or not used at all.

Flooring Tile is the hardest wearing, but cold. Carpet can retain strong aromas and stain easily. Wooden floors require careful maintenance and can be noisy. Consider a combination of all three for the different demands made by each area. The noise factor is important. Sometimes the deadened effect of a carpet and ceiling can create the wrong atmosphere; the hushed tones of an expensive doctor's waiting room do not make for a vibrant, enjoyable mood. A wooden floor does create some noise and can enhance the general clatter of conversation, music perhaps, and noises off such as corks being pulled or plates stacked in the kitchen. The use of different floor levels can create interest and sight lines.

Walls Beware of wallpaper and think of hygiene; consider the value of the chair rail; and decide the location of light fixtures and power points before finishing the surfaces.

Ceilings Decisions to be made include how high, and what form of lighting plot. Consider absorbent materials to cut down noise, and remember air conditioning considerations.

Heating and ventilation The choice of heating must be made early on: baseboard pipes take up the least space; portable paraffin heaters are out. Consult a specialist for heating and ventilation; it will save money later to have an effective system installed at the beginning.

Toilets In a new restaurant there is the opportunity to have a little fun with the toilets. Whatever the state of existing facilities, changes will inevitably be made. Restaurant toilets must always be clean and easily maintained. No sound should be heard in the dining room when the doors are closed. After that, the decorator can go to town. Having some fun can be a talking point when it comes to toilet decor. Why did the highest restaurant in Manhattan spend at least $2 million on its toilets? Strange pictures, full-length mirrors or wild colours can transform something mundane into a place worth keeping pristine, as well as being a conversation piece.

The kitchen

Whatever the layout of the kitchen, the chef ultimately has to make it work for producing the menu. A professional team which plans a kitchen would include an equipment company with its own planning department, the chef, the builder and the owner. On the other hand, the experienced owner with kitchen experience and a previous involvement in setting up restaurants, can tackle the job with second-hand items and an all-round builder/carpenter/plumber.

The kitchen flow Layouts must be planned to create efficient movement of incoming goods to storage areas; of goods from storage to preparation areas; of prepared items to service; and for easy disposal of waste at each stage. There are two further aspects of flow — the access from the kitchen to the dining room, and the flow areas within the kitchen where waiting staff must not interfere with preparation and cooking.

Constructional details There is plenty of advice available to the restaurateur concerning construction methods and the materials for professional kitchens: the most reliable source of information is the local Environmental Health Department. Great importance is attached to hygiene and maintenance, and the best way to ensure that the kitchen conforms to the standards laid down by law is to arrange for a visit before any constructional work begins.

Environmental Health Officers are keen to ensure that catering establishments work with the authority and not against them. The basic construction and the installation of equipment follow the law of common sense, reinforced with specific requirements for floor, wall and ceiling coverings, accurate refrigeration and general standards of hygiene for maintaining a clean operation.

In addition to statutory legislation concerning construction and operation of commercial establishments, at least one member of the kitchen team is expected to undergo a special hygiene training course recommended by the local Environmental Health Officer or the Hotel and Catering Training Board (HCTB). For a more complete understanding of the requirements and recommendations, read *Hygiene for Management* R Sprenger (Highfield Publications, 1989).

Fig 8 WORK FLOW DIAGRAM

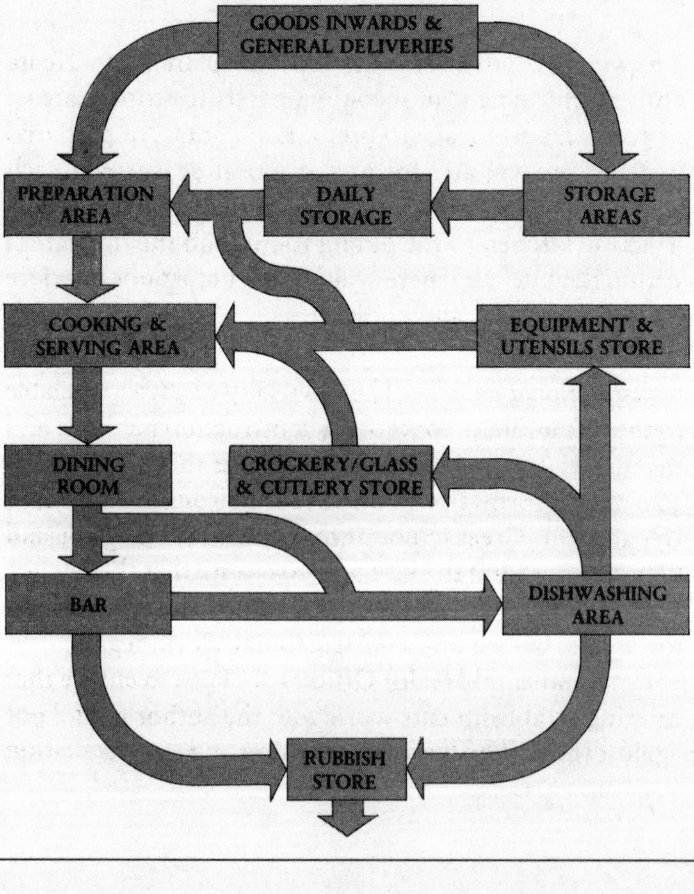

Kitchen planning and equipment The restaurant kitchen has to work with the equipment and staff to produce every item on the menu, and this production has to be consistent whether the restaurant is full or quiet.

While the professional planner is working with guidelines from the chef and incorporating statutory requirements, there are some considerations worth examining for a more efficient kitchen operation.

KITCHEN PLANNING POINTS

1. *Stoves and cooking facilities* The menu will dictate what stove is required. The combination of a solid-top oven with a four- or six-burner is the most popular core of the cooking area. With the addition of a grill, a deep-fat fryer, and a convection oven, nearly all types of cooking can be achieved.

   A source of water near the stove is highly recommended, and the necessary extraction should be planned to remove effectively the cooking odours, steam and smoke. Any large amounts of frying require more powerful forms of extraction. Lighting is also essential in the cooking area as are work surfaces and storage space for cooking equipment. The hanging pot rack releases valuable storage area, and if located near the cooking area provides the chef with extra space.

2. *Refrigeration* The maxim that warns that the more roads built the more cars there will be to fill them also applies to refrigeration. In the kitchen, refrigerators are invariably full and sensible planning will provide the right size in the appropriate area. The main requirement is for storage of perishable raw materials. The other and equally important need is for a fridge near to the cooking area to store finished items ready for cooking. A counter-top fridge or a 'low boy' can be used for this purpose. A work surface above a refrigerated unit provides a storage facility near the cooking process and can even be used in front of the cooking range as an integral part of the serving process. *See figure 9.*

   Some kitchens rely on freezers and microwaves, others on fresh materials and known cooking techniques. Whatever the inclination, a freezer is always essential whether for ice cream, emergencies, or storage of basics in the kitchen repertoire. The main freezer need not be sited in the immediate kitchen,

Fig 9 COUNTER REFRIGERATION IN THE COOKING AREA

the only requirement there being for the service of ices. Sometimes a mini freezer is used for this, and the main freezer located elsewhere.

Commercial refrigeration is far more durable than domestic units and considerably more expensive. If the refrigeration comes from a second-hand source, inspect it carefully. There are no equivalents of the AA in the restaurant business, but a local refrigerator repair man might be persuaded to check out prospective units. Compressors and thermostats are the two main delicate areas and when buying second-hand try to obtain guarantees for these parts. It is possible to run two or more refrigerated units from one compressor, but the danger is that should the compressor fail, all the fridges will stop. Built-in compressors for each unit increase the cost as well as the reliability.

3. *Preparation areas* The kitchen can be divided into preparation, service, and dishwashing areas. Preparation of the menu requires work surfaces, storage for food and equipment, and certain heavy items of equipment such as mixers, processors and other machines which need power sources, and space when not in use. Prep areas account for a diversity of functions: vegetables, fish, meat, poultry and desserts. The small restaurant has to compromise on space; larger operations merit separate areas for these different types of preparation.

4. *Service* Food which is ready to leave the kitchen must be kept at the appropriate temperature. Heated shelves, infra-red lamps or hot cupboards assist the service of hot food; keeping cold food away from the hot areas of the kitchen requires additional space. Remember that the coldness of a refrigerator is not the right temperature for service, and that a hot plate goes a long way in maintaining the heat of cooked items. Plates can be stored in a hot cupboard or simply on a shelf above the cooking range.

   When a waiter enters the kitchen, his first requirement is space to display the check, or order, he has taken for a specific table. The chef needs to refer to the check constantly and the checks must be arranged in sequence. This is the basis of communication between floor and kitchen.

   The ancillaries of food service, such as salads, bread and coffee, are best positioned away from the main serving. Every time the kitchen door opens it creates a minor distraction for the kitchen team. The priority in kitchen service is for the waiter to enter and exit with the minimum of disturbance, and to order or collect as efficiently as possible.

5. *Dishwashing* There are two types of washing up: one for pots and utensils, the other for plates, glasses and cutlery. Many restaurants use a machine for both; the alternative is to wash by hand. In either case, the dishwashing process is part of the kitchen and not a separate entity. Remember, the person employed as dishwasher is part of the kitchen team and needs to be visible.

   Statutory requirements are for a temperature of 77°C (170°F) to sterilise, or appropriate chemicals can be used. Provision has to be made in this area for storing dirty and clean equipment, cleaning agents and rubbish containers. The essentials here are the convenient location of the dishwashing

area which services both dining room and kitchen and adequate allocation of space for wet and dry rubbish.

Without an efficient washing-up system the whole operation can founder, so the process must be carefully planned not simply an afterthought. If the dishwasher cannot function for lack of equipment or storage space, every other area suffers. If possible, all cleaning agents and equipment should be kept in the same area.

The kitchen is the factory while the dining room is the sales office and showroom. With the increasing demand for variety in cooking styles and for freshly prepared ingredients, kitchen planning must allow for the flexible menu which will change during the life time of the restaurant, and the catering for larger groups, whether private parties in the restaurant or at locations elsewhere.

There is a need for certain paperwork in the kitchen: rotas, suppliers' lists, costings, a record of daily purchase and stock controls. A telephone is essential, combined, perhaps with an intercom system to the other areas of the establishment.

The cost of installing a kitchen can be substantially reduced if second-hand equipment is purchased sensibly, and the effectiveness of a working kitchen can be improved by bringing in the chef at the planning stage.

ANCILLARY DEPARTMENTS

These include:

- **The office: there is so much paperwork to contend with that provision of some office space should be thought about. Where space is at a premium the office can be located away from the restaurant, or the dining room can be used at off-peak times, although this is never a satisfactory solution.**
- **Staff changing rooms and toilets**
- **Clean uniform store**
- **Dry goods storage**

- **Vegetable storage**
- **Cold rooms and refrigerators**
- **Non-food storage: linen, stationery, cleaning materials, replacements, crockery, glass**
- **Wine and liquor storage**
- **Cleaning cupboard for vacuum cleaner, polisher, mops, buckets**

When looking at a space for a new restaurant, the ancillary areas are often forgotten; hence the importance of a cellar or a floor above. Hygiene regulations and general order demand that all aspects of the operation be thought about in the planning stages.

LIGHTING

Until recent times, lighting was not an important part of the designer's bag of tricks. Today, lighting is one of the first considerations, playing a large part in providing colour, atmosphere and tone. There are so many varieties of bulbs, fixtures and effects that lighting designers abound, often persuading their clients to spend more on lights than anything else in the decor of the dining room (and certainly increasing the maintenance budget with the bulb replacement costs).

Apart from its practical function, lighting is an integral part of the decor plan, with the aim of making the food look appetising and customers look appealing. Light fittings can also be chosen to act as decorative accessories.

Side lighting and up lighting flatter more than direct overhead light sources. Table-top lighting with a back-up of indirect lighting looks great but is only suitable for certain kinds of operation, those with spacious tables and a need for that particular effect.

The moods created by different intensities of light can be controlled with dimmers, while food can be made to look more colourful using coloured bulbs which bathe the dishes in a pool of soft pink rays. Mirrors used in conjunction with a planned lighting arrangement can add to the illusion of space and provide interest.

Lunch and dinner require separate approaches: the daylight should be as natural as possible, while at night the mood can alter as the evening progresses. And lighting can be used to influence behaviour: turning up all the lights will soon destroy the romantic moods of the last lingering diners and hurry them to the exit.

For reference, try noticing how players are lit on stage, or make friends with a good photographer and learn how clever lighting can enhance the plainest face or still life. Always remember the curse of overhead lighting and how it creates shadows where they shouldn't be. Flexibility can be achieved with track lighting and various spot- or flood-lights. Electric table lighting is the most rigid arrangement.

Kitchens with daylight are rare in city operations, the basement being a typical location. Fluorescent bulbs are popular in the working areas because they do not produce heat and are economical. A problem with them is when the kitchen door opens and the fluorescent glare spills out into the room, usually disturbing the mood set by softer dimmed lights.

Finally, the exterior needs illuminating to draw attention to the name and address, to light up the entrance and to enable the menu to be read; and all achieved with the neighbourhood in mind.

BUILDING AND INSTALLATION

Before construction or alterations begin, the cost and timing have to be established. Both factors are likely to change so make allowances, especially for an increase in cost. One important factor which affects the final price is any change made in the design after the work has begun, something which happens more often when the designer is an amateur. Changes can also create delays in the work, and sometimes a penalty clause can be introduced to ensure that the project is completed in time for the planned opening. Conversely, an incentive can be offered to achieve an earlier completion.

There is a certain order of work in any construction, and builders have their own methods which seem to defy any logical progress. The first stage is to plot the lines of power, water, heating, ventilation and lighting, then comes the construction, followed by decoration.

Knowledge of the constructional details is useful for future maintenance and repairs. The location of pipes, fuses and plumbing needs to be known, and it could be useful if at least one member of staff becomes handy with repairs, to avoid costly call-outs for simple tasks.

Professional catering equipment can require specialist installers and, again, some member of staff should become familiar with the operation of each item. Suppliers will, or certainly should, offer free training for the operators of all equipment. Insist that as many people as possible understand how everything works.

No wonder so many restaurants are designed by their owners. One of the chief attractions in becoming a restaurant owner is the satisfaction of spending money (not necessarily your own) on a design which reflects your taste. There is a definite reward for the designer when the project is completed and the result gains objective compliments from staff and customers alike.

Turning an ordinary shop into a thriving restaurant is an art and needs great experience, with an eye for colour, proportion and detail. Restaurants are places for people — to sit, talk, eat and drink, to be seen, to show off, to flirt. This provides the brief for restaurant design.

Good restaurant design allows people to be seen and be comfortable. Bad design ignores people and tries to be something other than a restaurant, an extravagant fantasy of the designer's at the client's expense.

Function with beauty: the restaurant's purpose is to serve food and drink, not to idolise itself. Seats should support their occupants comfortably, lights should illuminate the guests flatteringly, and the tables should be set spaciously. People provide the decor with their dress, their animation, and their personalities. An empty restaurant looks empty and no amount of cluttering with artefacts can compensate for poor business.

CHAPTER FOUR

THE KITCHEN

With the finance sound, the location secured, the alterations completed, and the legal requirements met (*see page 146* ***Legal Checklist***) the restaurant is set to open. How does this all get pulled together? How do you get to that moment when the door opens for the first time to the public?

Without any experienced employees at the pre-opening stage there is no hope of an orderly start; it will be a bumpy passage for a few months until some semblance of routine appears. The first-time owner must engage professional experience, if only for initial consultancy.

The hiring of the chef, if the proprietor is inexperienced, can be the most difficult of all the initial problems in setting up. Look through the pages of *Caterer and Hotelkeeper* or local classifieds where there are always long lists of establishments in search of chefs. To borrow from a familiar source, 'first find your chef', for with the experienced chef comes knowledge of kitchen management and the skills of training and purchasing.

PURCHASING

The key to a profitable kitchen operation is skill in buying and allowing time for purchasing to be undertaken in a way that secures quality and high profit. Setting up the purchasing procedures begins with lists based on the menu, and for each list another with names of suppliers, their prices and telephone numbers.

Purchasing happens on a daily, weekly and monthly basis. The organised kitchen maintains a constant supply of non-perishable items, and usually stocks up monthly from a regular supplier on a delivery basis. Alternative sources for dry goods would be the Cash and Carry, supermarket or the manufacturer direct. These are the items which arrive first in the new kitchen — a good chance to see if the ideas on storage and access work.

On a weekly basis the semi-perishables are bought, items such as eggs, most dairy products, root vegetables and certain fruits — another opportunity to test various suppliers. It can be worthwhile visiting the nearest wholesale market if there is one within reasonable distance, especially when buying fresh produce. Within these markets there are dramatic price fluctuations and competition between traders makes for some interesting comparisons.

A regular check with the market can give a good guide to prices and allow for knowledgeable bargaining when dealing with a middleman.

At the other end of the supply line comes the local retailer and there is some goodwill benefit in giving the butcher and greengrocer some business, and a local fishmonger is a godsend. Negotiate whatever discount possible and maybe suggest a free meal to get the ball rolling. Encouraging local traders in the community can only enhance the restaurant's business and your reputation as a genial host. However, even with 10 or 15 per-cent discount, the local retailer cannot compete with a more direct form of supply.

The most popular source of supplies is the wholesaler. The system is made easy for the buyer with telephone ordering, taped messages in the middle of the night and delivery the next day. The advantage of knowing the voice at the end of the line and the time saved in deliveries can outweigh the cost difference; this is where bargaining and comparison shopping techniques are used.

There are many suppliers for every aspect of kitchen

purchase who are competing for more business. Shopping around and using quotes fom one supplier to another takes time, but on a weekly basis there is always a slot (afternoons can be the easiest time for the chef). Never take the printed list as anything other than fiction. It is a guide, and all prices for food supplies can be challenged or found lower elsewhere. Restaurant suppliers want all of your business within the range of food they sell. However, to get locked into one supplier, the fish order for example, can be dangerous especially if you are on a credit system. Certain suppliers will encourage this and let months go by without pressing for payment, only to turn round later and start hefty price increases and even credit charges. Slipping behind in regular food bills reaps a grim harvest for the unsuspecting buyer.

Daily purchases are concerned with the most perishable items and this is where the money can disappear through over-ordering, waste, fraud, and in last minute panic ordering. The first weeks in a restaurant's life are completely unpredictable, whether it starts with hefty publicity and a splashy opening or a mute arrival into the world without any prior warning. Whichever the case, the menu must be served in its entirety every session. How else can you begin? A reviewer comes for lunch one day and for dinner the following week, writes a piece in the local weekly, and the neighbourhood starts to trickle in. To start greeting new arrivals with 'I'm sorry it's off', smacks of amateur farce backed up by no conviction.

Purchasing for the opening period has to be a combination of restraint and psychic intuition. A small menu helps but it cannot be too small. While flexibility with the lunch menu is one way of helping with waste, an empty dining room and a fridge full of goodies can be typical in the early days.

It is quite in order to buy limited amounts of perishables and to state that something is no longer being offered.

'Everyone has been ordering it', or 'The chef wasn't happy with the quality of the Seychelles parrot fish today', have been heard in places where the paint was still drying. The way to complete the story is to offer something else and not deplete the diners' choice.

The opening period can be used for entertaining, bringing in those retailers from the neighbourhood, or trading a meal for two for some installation work by a local plumber. Friends of the staff could come and eat for a discount, the nearest to rent-a-crowd you can get. Whatever tactics are tried, there is always the dilemma in the opening months of to buy or not to buy. The chef has to work closely with the manager/owner and they must make the decisions collectively until some pattern of business emerges.

SOME POINTS ON PURCHASING

- **Try to find new sources of supply: local farmers, game farms, local co-ops; or try to get growers in the area to produce specifics for your operation. Think about bulk purchases with other establishments, remembering that discounts are available in proportion to the amounts bought.**
- **Get to know the wholesalers and develop contacts; ask them for recommendations; invite them to eat at your establishment after you have seen their operation. Look out for suppliers who deliver to other establishments in your area. Use the cheque book wherever possible and record on the counterfoil in detail. Beware of using too much cash, although deals for cash mean more bargaining power. Get receipts, or record the transaction. Use the means of making regular payments to bring the price down. Compare case prices at local supermarkets with the Cash and Carry remembering time and distance.**
- **Always have a set of scales near the entrance for deliveries and check weights when orders arrive. Make sure the delivery man sees the items being weighed and inspected. Check date stamps, especially for dairy items. Remember the grades of produce, and whether the best quality is always needed.**

There are advantages in buying whole items, whether meat or fish on the bone, cases or sacks, but check there is enough storage and waste disposal. Reliable deliveries and the timing of ordering to catch the deliveries is crucial.

- **Haggle, barter, cajole and stick to your guns. Never accept the first price, and shop around for bargains.**
- **What incentives are there for the chef to save money on purchases? Keeping a record of the chef's kitchen profit makes any incentive more visible.**
- **Develop contacts at the local pubs; the landlords can be a mine of information.**
- **Think about a trip to France or Belgium, a day out for the staff on a bleak Sunday in March to stock up for spring.**

Purchasing need not be the recital into a machine at midnight, and time spent on purchasing can enhance profitability and involve the whole kitchen team.

THE KITCHEN TEAM

There are three essential aspects of the chef's skills: cooking, buying, and teaching. Kitchens are training schools for the chefs, not showcases for temperamental stars. The creation of a working team inspired by a communicative leader at the stove is the objective when aiming for constancy and consistency.

The vagabond nature of some chefs leads to many disappointments and frustrations in the early days of restaurants without owner chefs. Tempted by better money, they leave the protection of an established operation to become leaders themselves. A few weeks later they walk out in the middle of service declaring your place not good enough for their talents, and back they go to the previous employer.

Youth and enthusiasm are attractive features to employ, but can youth train, and does enthusiasm buy sensibly? Establishing a working team in the kitchen is the chef's first responsibility and without trained help the chef will have to produce the menu single-handed with raw recruits looking on.

Finding kitchen help is one impossible task and keeping them is another. Finding the right staff is both time consuming and frustrating. School leavers, college students, part-timers as well as life's flotsam are found in new kitchens; or partners' wives, lovers, children and au pairs. There can be an international flavour; visiting antipodeans culled from ads in their free sheets have been a fruitful source for some kitchens I have come across.

The lack of a labour pool can be the severest handicap for any new business, and especially for the labour-intensive kitchen. Ideally, recruit a youngish local crew who want to learn and have incentives to stay, a decent wage being one of the prime motivations.

The chef must have a say in the hiring; it is unfair and self-defeating to foist the first one through the door on an unwilling master. Often the unsullied mind is the easiest to train. Training a novice means applying the techniques and methods relevant to the restaurant's menu, and previous training in a kitchen with cruder methods can hamper the new skills being learnt. Also, the chef will be more patient with a novice. Harshness is usually aimed at those who, it is felt, should know better. It can be easier to hire a dish-washer than a kitchen assistant, and they often make the best trainees — after all, where else is there for them to go other than up.

If there are more recruits available, hire them too and train the best. Dishwashers (or kitchen porters for the grander types) can come from a multitude of backgrounds none of them having any connection with the kitchen, and this can be to their advantage. After a few weeks of greasy pots nothing could be better than peeling carrots or stringing beans.

Using two porters or more, the dishwashing becomes

a shared effort and the cooking tasks can be swapped. Strengths emerge in different areas; some better with pastry, others who go for sauces. By starting with the dishwashing, the importance of that position is recognised because it is the link between kitchen and floor and supplies the restaurant's wherewithal to serve.

Keep the dishwasher but increase his tasks and vary them. Build up the repertoire of preparation and elevate the truly gifted to the dizzy heights of stove and grill work. True chefs will emerge, sometimes employing techniques without understanding what makes the dish work. Never mind, that can come later.

Begin the training by familiarising the students with the basics. The knife comes first. Some beginners are petrified of a sharp knife. A student at a cookery school will begin by turning vegetables or chopping for a mirepoix. Endless carrots transformed into batons or perfectly squared potatoes bring confidence with the knife. I have seen students holding a carrot and treating it as an extension of their finger, fearful of cutting it, or peeling a potato slowly and lovingly. There is no time for such delicate flowers in the professional kitchen. Speed, and developing efficiency with the mundane, is the essence.

Develop techniques of vegetable, fruit and salad preparation, and let speeds develop before moving to the next stages. As recruits become more used to handling equipment and materials, let them work with the chef at the stove for short periods during service, to grasp the sort of speed and reactions required, and then put them back to the string beans.

The first time at the stove in a real service period should inspire enough to speed up the basic skills and appreciate the pressure and atmosphere of the kitchen experience. As confidence grows, start teaching taste and how to identify flavourings. Making stock is a good way to illustrate the power of reduction, the use of herbs and aromatics, the strength of salt, and the effect of alcohol. Tasting at every stage is something a student should always do, while the experienced chef rarely needs to.

When teaching the actual cooking processes, explain why certain methods are used and illustrate by tasting and testing. The change of colour or texture, for example, can be indicated. The technique of stopping the cooking process in vegetables, refreshing and reheating to achieve the correct crunch and colour is a good way to introduce trainees to the skills of taste and texture.

It is essential to get the flavourings and seasonings correct; that is what gives a kitchen its identity, the special difference which is noticed and relied on for consistency. Techniques are easily taught but passing on tastebuds is more difficult. Taste can be taught by introducing flavours and building up the repertory of seasonings. Start apprentices in this final training by cooking staff meals, not experimenting on customers. Staff are the best critics.

Learning to plan the order of preparation can be done when the team is familiar with the basic skills; good food comes about through the correct order of preparation, which ensures that items are prepared to the point of finishing off and assembly.

The menu is prepared by performing tasks in a distinct order, bearing in mind what is available from the previous service and what has to be prepared for the next day. It makes no sense to start at the beginning of the menu and work through to the end. Pastry needs a certain period and a cool space, sauces take time to reduce and deepen in flavour. Reckoning how long a dish takes to prepare only becomes meaningful when the team is making it in real operation not in a pre-opening trial. The skilled chef plans at least two or three days ahead while allowing for flexibility, and lets the team know what tasks need to be done and in what order.

Accurate costings must be undertaken constantly in the

Fig 10

A TYPICAL STAFF ROTA FOR A FIFTY-SEATER RESTAURANT

	Monday	Tuesday	Wednesday	Thursday	Friday	Saturday
Chef	8am–12noon 6pm–11pm	10am– 2pm 6pm–10pm	10am– 2pm 6pm–10pm	10am– 2pm 6pm–10pm	10am– 2pm 6pm–10pm	10am– 2pm 6pm–11pm
Kitchen Assistant	8am– 5pm	8am– 5pm	8am– 5pm	8am– 5pm	8am– 5pm	8pm– 5pm
Dishwasher*	8am– 4pm	8am– 4pm	8am– 4pm	8am– 4pm	8am– 4pm	8am– 4pm
Dishwasher*	5pm–12pm	5pm–12pm	5pm–12pm	5pm–12pm	5pm–12pm	5pm–12pm
Manager	9am– 3pm 6pm–12pm	9am– 3pm 6pm–12pm	9am– 3pm 6pm–12pm	9am– 3pm 6pm–12pm	9am– 3pm 6pm–12pm	9am– 3pm 6pm–12pm
Waiter 1	10am– 4pm	10am– 4pm	10am– 4pm	10am– 4pm	10am– 4pm	10am– 4pm
Waiter 2	5pm–12pm	5pm–12pm	5pm–12pm	5pm–12pm	5pm–12pm	5pm–12pm
Waiter 3	— —	— —	— —	12noon–3pm 6pm–12pm	12noon–3pm 6pm–12pm	12noon–3pm 6pm–12pm
Busboy	10am– 4pm	10am– 4pm	10am– 4pm	10am– 4pm	10am– 4pm	10am– 4pm
Busboy	5pm–12pm	5pm–12pm	5pm–12pm	5pm–12pm	5pm–12pm	5pm–12pm
Bartender	11am– 3pm 6pm– 1am	— —	— —	11am– 3pm 6pm–12pm	11am– 3pm 6pm–12pm	11am– 3pm 6pm– 1am
Bookkeeper**				10am– 4pm		

* Alternate Sunday cleaning 12 noon–4 pm.
Waiter 3 is part-time.
Bartender has two full days off where manager fills in at bar.
Staff rotation at manager's discretion.
Weekly cleaning on Sundays.
**Bookkeeper makes one weekly visit and one monthly visit.

opening period to make sure that the right amount of mark-up is being used, and that portions are in line, and to keep in touch with current prices. The technique of portion control and costing out each dish can be taught, providing that the need for accurate costings has been proved.

Ideally, for large establishments, the chef needs a secretary because there is a considerable amount of paperwork to get through. Stocktaking, keeping records of purchases and sales, rotas, purchase lists and ordering; all these functions bring paper into the kitchen. Certain restaurants require the chef to cook all the time so that the clerical details must be looked after by the manager or partner in the front.

Initially, everyone will work flat out for all hours and there is no such luxury as regular working shifts. But a rota establishes the structure of working hours in the kitchen, and needs careful planning to account for split shifts, cleaning, and extra staff at busier times, particularly when attempting lunch and dinner six days a week. Try not to pay overtime, but give staff time off in lieu, or the unexpected day off. You must treat your staff well, they are your lifeblood.

The kitchen record should be maintained in such a way that a complete stranger could arrive if the chef goes astray and take over the running. It should include telephone numbers of suppliers and staff, recipes and purchase lists, and emergency numbers for repairs and maintenance, as well as columns recording purchases, sales, and kitchen labour to get a daily analysis of the kitchen profit.

Restaurant chefs are more than simply chefs, they need managerial skills, leadership qualities, and the right response to an urgent situation. There must be discipline in the kitchen, especially when it comes to hygiene and regular cleaning.

Restaurant cooking is hard work, harder if the chef does

not appreciate the reasons for thorough preparation and record keeping. Chefs have to develop a structure to work in, to recognise their strong points and listen about their weak ones. The importance of neat and organised paperwork has to be recognised by the most undisciplined artistic genius at the stove. Too often the example of wild chefs braying at their team, spending more time in garnishing than preparing, can become the copied stereotype. Temperament becomes more important than leadership and the resulting misery spills out into the dining room. To achieve good food it isn't necessary to keep some wild, exotic animal pacing up and down in the confines of the kitchen; benevolent autocracy is preferable to manic undisciplined rage.

Ultimately, the chef needs to understand about money and controls. There should be some involvement in the financial running of the whole operation for the chef to keep the wage cost within budget, to keep replacements and repairs to the minimum, and to buy well. Hiring agency staff at the drop of a toque, calling out Hobart to change a fuse, or buying fillet steak from the local butcher in a moment of panic are common where chefs have no sense of financial responsibility or involvement with management.

The kitchen operation should begin as it means to continue; introducing controls, discipline, and mis en place procedures will enable the chef to have time to train his staff, to create new dishes, and to develop a steady pace of work.

Pulling a team together to launch a new menu in an untested kitchen is a tremendous effort and a great responsibility. There will always be times of panic and crisis. It is how the chef and his team respond that determines success in getting food out which is consistent and accurate. There can be nothing more enjoyable for the chef in the restaurant than being at the stove, with a full board of checks, everything prepared for efficient service and the team moving together at dazzling speed, producing food they enjoy making and serving. The timing works, the waiters return the empty plates, and the kitchen flows on a mixture of adrenalin, satisfaction and sweat.

CHAPTER FIVE

THE DINING ROOM

Thoughtful preparation determines the quality of food in the kitchen and this applies equally to efficient and professional service in the dining room.

The front-of-house differs primarily in that it is a public domain and has to be maintained in a constant state of readiness. The first task and the last when setting up a room for service is cleaning. Just as the chef trains and prepares his team, so the manager has responsibility for the dining room. Even an experienced crew takes weeks to get everything right and in its place. The initial weeks of service by an amateur group can be a nightmare and there is only so much naivety that a customer can take. The secret of the organised dining room is to hire experience.

One of the first tasks is to make the layout work, or to adapt it for easy service. This is a critical point directly affecting income and the capacity of the dining room must adhere to the original projections. Missing two covers with an average spend of £20 could represent a loss of £10,000 a year. It is up to the manager and the waiters to test the layout and make changes with dummy runs.

To illustrate the amount of work involved in setting up the dining room, think what it is like to entertain at home on a single occasion — a three-course meal with aperitifs, wines and liqueurs, for example, where the guests are all business contacts from overseas and their approval of the occasion could enhance the host's income. Time is spent preparing the whole house, with fresh flowers, clean towels, hoovered carpets, cleaned windows, polished silverware and glasses, ice, nibbles with drinks, clean ashtrays, clean napkins and laundered and ironed table cloth, and some gentle background music perhaps. There is no mention of any cooking yet, and this is only a partial list of the work involved in setting up for six guests in a private house. Now multiply that by eight or 10 and you begin to have an idea of the responsibilities of the restaurant manager. The waiters or bar staff should do all the restaurant, bar and public cloakroom cleaning. Hire a part-time cleaner and everything will be left for this one person to do.

At home the easy part is the food since six guests in a private dining room will not be ordering off a menu. There is little waste in private catering when you are certain of the numbers and the menu. This illustrates how important skilful order-taking is in a restaurant.

The layout works and the room is clean: now comes the business of getting the dining room to a state of readiness for service. Tables are planned to accommodate reservations for the forthcoming session and care is needed to supervise this part of the set up. The whole room is set up rather than individual tables at a time. It is far easier to carry 14 stem glasses in one hand, and safer than using a tray. Also, carrying 20 knives in a napkin with the blades down, and giving a quick polish as each one is laid, gets the job done more quickly than setting each table individually. Condiments are checked all at once and then placed. All the table top items, flowers, ashtrays, candles, are treated in the same manner.

The accompaniments to the menu are prepared and brought to a suitable serving point; cold sauces, butter, cream, sugar, bread, coffee, all the ancillaries prepared for immediate service.

The allocation of tables can be a sensitive operation. There are always certain tables which are better than others, and waiters have an instinct for them. Waiters prefer larger groups of people which mean bigger bills usually producing bigger tips. A proficient waiter can handle at least five tables (say 20 people) and even more with the assistance of a junior, runner, or commis. It can depend on the simplicity of the menu and food presentation, and the amount of work done by the manager in the dining room, whether the order is taken by the manager or the table is left completely to the control of the waiter at a particular station.

Another important allocation is the issuing of check pads. For effective control the orders should be taken on serialised checks, triplicated and pre-carboned. The beginning of each pad is recorded against the waiter's name and missing checks must be accounted for. The top copy goes to the kitchen, the next to the cash desk, bar, or till and the third remains with the waiter. Restaurant checks are the same as bank cheques. They are exchanged for food and drink, which is money for the restaurant, and every transaction should be treated in this way.

The storing of checks and the making up of bills needs close attention. Does the waiter write up a guest's bill or does the cashier, manager or bartender? Bills are needed as soon as they are asked for, in a legible form which is easy to check and is representative of the whole style of operation. In terms of security, the writing of the bill should be performed by the person responsible for the cash flow, usually the owner.

While computerisation has eliminated much of the paper and time taken up in writing bills, there are still ways of abusing the system. Is a computer really financially viable? Remember the intricacies and knowledge required for their operation. It would be wise for the novice to understand the manual approach to restaurant controls before deciding to opt for the computer which does everything except cook.

Other pieces of paper needed for service are bills, credit slips and menus. *See Chapter 2* ***Restaurant Finances***.

The use of a check rack separates the checks into slots for each table number and allows the cashier to select the information for each table. By establishing the system of exchanging checks for goods from day one, bills can be written without asking each waiter what wines table three had, or whether table six had coffee.

With the paperwork in order, there is a series of routine checks to make before the doors open. If there is a cloth operation, linen supplies should be checked every two days. Professional laundries are notorious for losing, destroying and forgetting, their deliveries can be erratic, and it seems they would much prefer the restaurant to hire tablecloths and napkins. Running out of cloth napkins happens all the time and the trick is to maintain a hidden supply for emergencies, or wash your own, or use paper. Laundry service is expensive and can be out of proportion to other running costs, so if there is the space and a person to do it, launder on site. The abuse of linen in a restaurant is often a nagging and costly problem and the decision about linen may very well change as business increases and stocks decrease.

The other costly abuse in the dining room is with the table top supplies, either by staff or by customer. The initial choice of plate, cutlery and glassware will affect their longevity. Stylish establishments opt for large objects. A solid piece of silver (albeit plate), larger-volume glasses to enhance bouquet and colour, the decorative cover plate at least 10 inches in diameter, the oversized napkin indicating the luxury of ample linen to cover and protect, all say largesse.

The small, the flimsy and the thin indicate something less. Problems occur when small restaurants choose large objects without the space to store them or the care needed to protect them from breakage or theft.

As the time of opening approaches the final details are checked: flowers, light levels, music, the menu, and any final alterations made. The chef gives a run-down of the evening specials and the items which need a special push. A blackboard in the kitchen is useful to alert the waiters about the state of the kitchen. It can be used to alert waiters about the number of portions left of a special dish, and announce replacements for items no longer available. Toilets are given a thorough check. There is a final waiters' briefing on the menu by the chef (very important) and a word about any important clients. Staff with theatrical experience have an advantage when they work in restaurants because there is the same importance of mis en scène, the anticipation which builds through the last minute checking until the moment when the curtain rises and the shows begins.

Greeting and seating are the first encounters with the diners, best performed by the manager with the waiter taking over at table. Policy about who takes the order ensures an orderly approach, whether it is the manager or the waiter, because this is the most important moment of all and determines the profit more or less from the outset.

Fig 11

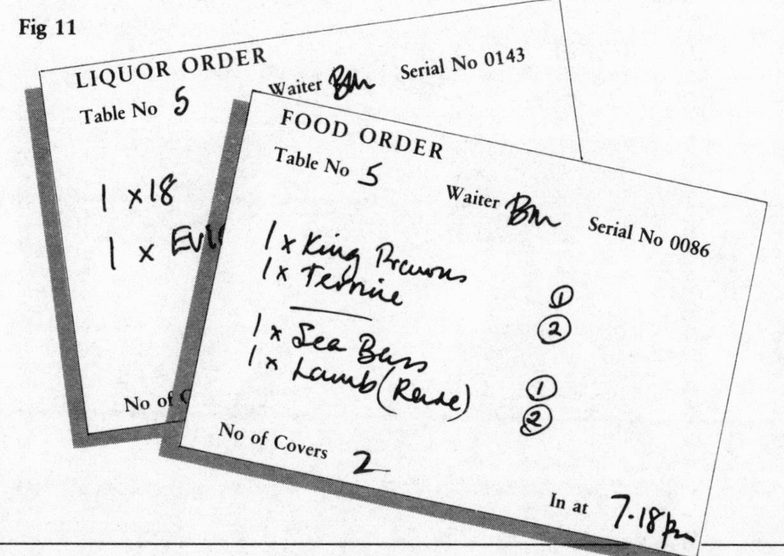

At this point it is appropriate to stress the balance of the menu and its variety of dishes, not rest content with an order of four smoked salmon starters followed by four duck dishes. For any retail operation, the point of sale is all important, and menu choice and orders taken at the table have to be recognised as vital in a restaurant. It goes without saying that orders should be written legibly in capitals, containing all the relevant information for the chef and the waiter.

All the information must be available to the chef and to the cashier: the number of covers; the time of entry in the kitchen; the waiter's name; any special instructions; and a number system which identifies who gets what.

A logical way of avoiding the dreaded 'whose soup is this?' style of service is by using the diner who is nearest the kitchen door as number one, writing his choice of dish at the top of the order, then progressing in a clockwise direction.

A walk through the dining room identifying the number one position at each table gives the waiter the opportunity to establish the system and agree the various numbers.

Drink orders are treated in the same manner identifying, for example, the person at the table who will taste the wine by using the number system again.

Fig 12 TABLE NUMBERING FOR IDENTIFYING CUSTOMERS

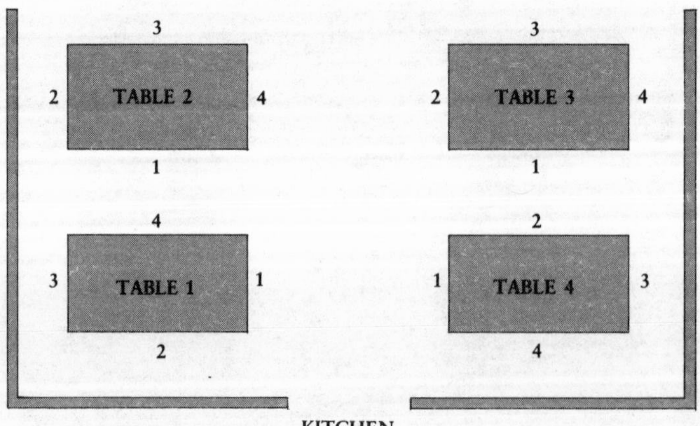

Whatever the style of service, there are certain aspects of waiting which should be remembered to create a consistent service, comfortable for the guest and the waiter.

SOME BASICS OF PROFESSIONAL WAITING

- **Hold a plate by using four fingers underneath and the thumb on the side of the rim, not touching the actual surface of the plate.**
- **Serve food from the left and clear from the right.**
- **Serve drinks from the right, which is where the glass is sited on the table.**

Fig 13 HOLDING A PLATE FOR SERVICE

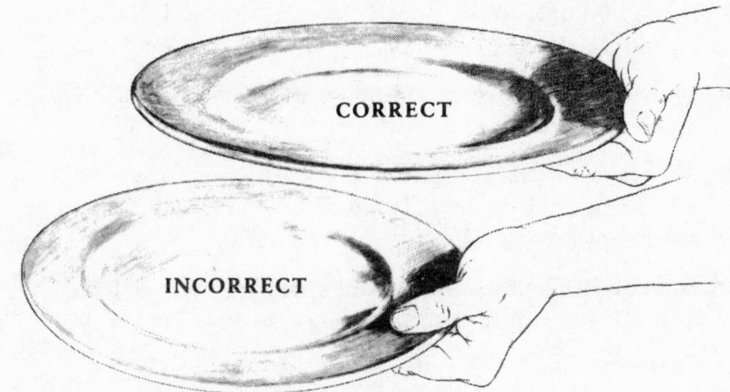

HOLDING MORE THAN ONE PLATE FOR SERVICE

CLEARING PLATES

Fig 14 SPOON AND FORK SERVICE

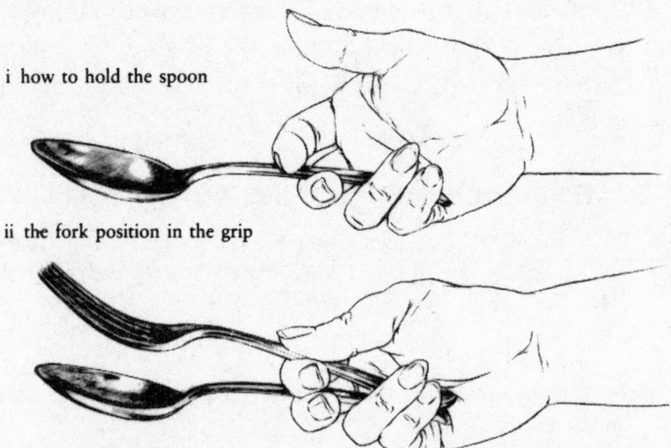

- Use spoon and fork service, silver service, where appropriate. It is useful practice if the staff have to wait at larger parties or outside catering functions.
- Clear the table after each stage of the meal, leaving it set for the next course.
- Always try to ensure that the place setting is covered with something until the meal is finished for everyone. An empty space looks unfriendly.
- Hold glasses by their stems, use a tray to clear, or better, take off two at a time to a serving station.
- Correct posture of a waiter at the table is standing erect, balanced properly, hands anywhere but pockets.
- The importance of waiters' dress: is the uniform functional as well as complementing the style and the time of service? The importance of personal hygiene: nails, shoes, hair and no aromas from any source (smokers beware; and remember that aftershave and perfumes do not belong where there are so many aromas and tastes to be recognised).
- Remember the importance of timing a meal. Allow time for the order to be produced and give the kitchen an idea of the timing required, for example the pause while aperitifs are being drunk.

There are two basic types of service, plated or silver; the kitchen arranges everything on the plate and the waiter transports it to the customer; or the food is placed on a serving platter, a plate at the appropriate temperature is set down, the waiter brings the serving platter and using a spoon and fork transfers the preparation to the plate. Vegetables and sauces are treated in the same way.

A compromise version of silver service is often employed when the main item is plated while the accompanying details are served by hand separately.

Whichever style works best for the menu, communication is the lynch pin of getting the right food to the right customer in the appropriate time frame. The check provides the link between kitchen and floor.

Many French operations borrow from the classic traditions of preparation and service to good effect, especially with the system of checks and order. The flimsy last copy of the triplicate pad is attached to the table, usually by the clip holding the paper covering over the linen cloth (another idea to consider when looking at laundry costs). In this way, every waiter can assist each other if a station is overloaded and help is needed. A new waiter coming to an unfamiliar table can immediately see what stage the meal is at by looking at the check and noticing the state of the cutlery on the table. (The disadvantage of this otherwise excellent scheme is that customers have been known to scribble on the check, spill wine over it, or make it disappear.)

In addition to the service and its supervision there are more responsibilities for the manager. Keeping up with the bills can take a fair amount of time during service. A bill is often written up as the customer is taking his chair, with the date, number of covers and pre-meal drinks. As the meal progresses appropriate entries are made, storing the bill in the check rack along with the various slips for drinks, food, coffee and extras. In a busy establishment with more than 50 covers computerisation of bills, with a built-in program for stock control, percentages and a break-down for each table, are the norm rather than the exception.

A manual system gives the novice a chance to examine individual orders and provides a feel for each session. At the end of each session, the bills have to be added up and analysed in a form similar to *figure 15*.

With all the information about the income and expenditure of the session the ordering can be done for the next day; the money is banked, the float is made up and another set of figures is ready for entry into the financial record.

While training takes place constantly in the kitchen, in the dining room there must be times for training other than during actual service. For the opening period a daily run through the serving techniques will be necessary for an inexperienced waiting staff. Again, this is where the professional is needed if only for the first few months, in a consultancy role if not part of the management team. There can be great satisfation for a restaurant owner and partners to pass on their professional skills to a group of previously inexperienced help, to watch the results and hold their enthusiasm.

Skills in waiting only develop through constant practice and benevolent training. Attack the problem of unskilled help by allowing them to work in the dining room on the trail of another, as the fetch and carry person. After trying some of the basics at a familiar table, teach one of the more complicated manoeuvres before or after service. Clearing plates in a slick way without the rattle, or worse, is one of the hallmarks of the experienced waiter; confident handling of the spoon and fork is another.

Knowledge of how the menu is prepared is necessary for the waiter to describe dishes adequately; it is not enough simply to taste. The benefits of swapping staff between kitchen and floor duties raises awareness of each department's contribution, provides knowledgeable

Fig 15

THE DAILY CASH SUMMARY

DATE:

IN	£	p
Cash till inc. cigarettes		
Payment by account customers		
Credit card payments		
Other payments in		
Sub-total		
Over		
Total		

OUT	£	p
Less cigarettes		
Charge cards: Access		
Amexco		
Barclaycard		
Diners		
Signed bills or A/C customers		
To bank		
Casual wages		
Cash food		
Cash sundries		
Cash wine		
Other items paid		
Sub-total		
Shorts		
Total		

substitutes in emergencies and assists the integrated approach to management.

The weekly rota should make allowance for swapping roles as well as providing staff to set up, staff to clear after service, and time for major cleaning tasks. Staggered shifts allow a smooth transition from lunch to dinner and can help to bring the wage cost down.

The use of casual help and staff from agencies will only add to the wage bill and bring in an extra level of confusion. Regular part-timers are often an essential aspect of the team; it is the last minute panic decision to pull in more staff at agency rates which can disastrously affect the wage bill. For the consistency which is vital to success, try to build up a pool of labour, part-time or full-time, which can be called on for a regular amount of work and training.

The constancy of staff in the dining room, their recognition by regular clients and their familiarity with the procedures and menu occurs in establishments where there is a respect for the skills and professionalism of waiting and where the management policies on wages and conditions (especially tips) attract staff and retain their loyalty.

Responsibility for the reservations book and telephone lie with the manager. Where there is a need for a reservation system, there is more chance of planning the session successfully while possibly increasing the amount of business. Keeping a record shows the pattern of business over a certain period and the number of covers served at each session. Regular clients are gleaned from this diary and walk-in business (they did not telephone or book, just arrived) is also recorded.

A session can be divided into sittings to maximise the amount of business. Special instructions can be written up for a particular party. A copy of the menu for each session should also be incorporated into the diary.

Fig 16

A PAGE FROM A RESERVATIONS BOOK

TABLE PLAN *(no. of seats in italics)*

1	2	3	4	5	6	7	8
(4/6)	*(4)*	*(4)*	*(4/6)*	*(2/3)*	*(2/3)*	*(2/3)*	*(2/3)*

BOOKINGS

Name	No. of covers	Time	Table no.	Tel. no.	Remarks

SEATING TIMES – LUNCH

No.	12.00noon–1.15pm	No.	1.15pm–2.30pm
1		1	
2		2	
3		3	
4		4	
5		5	
6		6	
7		7	
8		8	

SEATING TIMES – DINNER

No.	7.00pm–9.30pm	No.	9.30pm–11.00pm
1		1	
2		2	
3		3	
4		4	
5		5	
6		6	
7		7	
8		8	

The diary must be carefully maintained for legibility and everyone in the restaurant must be able to understand the system and what table and what times can be sold. A table plan shows the availability and notes can be left for the next session. Reservations must be made in pencil.

There is an art in plotting reservations in a busy restaurant, balancing the times and the spaces available, gauging the amount of time a party will take up, whether to overbook, the ability to persuade the potential customer to arrive earlier or later to balance the numbers at the right times, the courage to say no. Skills in planning reservations derive from the practices of large busy operations but are equally effective in the small 30-seat operation. It is important to achieve the maximum potential from a limited number of seats, and this is where the use of two definite seating times can be a distinct advantage.

In the early days of establishing systems and preparation schedules, certain habits and attitudes can develop. These are generally the result of the staff treating the restaurant as an extension of their own home, and whilst this can make for a convivial atmosphere it can also bring indulgences such as meals, drinks and telephone calls on the house. Curbing such behaviour is essential for cost control and the establishment of a structure which enables the work to be achieved in a pleasant manner. Think of the likely abuses and decide on some basic rules and regulations. These should be outlined at the interview stage and the reaction of applicants will be a good measure of their suitability. Whether to charge full price for beverages and off-duty staff meals, smoking, lateness, telephone calls, tips, breakages and uniforms, are some of the points to consider, and realise that in every case there will be some form of abuse.

The best way of understanding how successful operations work is either to become employed by them or to hire their expertise. Nothing beats the experience of waiting in a busy restaurant with a good control system and skilled styles of service. Banqueting experience will teach speeds and elementary techniques, and kitchen practice provides a greater understanding of timing and product.

New restaurants are judged by their all-round consistency. Proficient service takes time to develop during the 'shake down period'. To eliminate some of the elementary mistakes employ professionalism, establish a structure, and train constantly. Practise with friends and relatives to gain serving experience before unleashing amateurs on the public. Realise how important supervised preparation and cleaning are in establishing the structure for the busier dining room of the future.

PSYCHOLOGY AND THE DINING ROOM

Why do people eat out? What is there about sharing one of life's essential bodily functions with a bunch of strangers looking on?

Hunger and thirst, combined with the satisfaction that others prepare, serve and clean, form the background to a whole host of other more subtle and strange motivations. On one level there is vanity — showing off clothes, jewellery or companions; on another, the desire to indulge in social stimulation — flirting, making conquests, holding court with a regular group. There are the entertaining businessmen exhibiting their refined knowledge of wines and cigars, treating waiters with cool disdain, the role of master and servant played for the audience.

Clandestine meetings occur in restaurants; celebrities pick places to be noticed, feigning annoyance at being recognised. Some people eat out to be chastised, others to punish, both in the hope that a parent figure will take charge during the meal, an element missed in a deprived childhood. Some delight in embarrassing as many as possible with behaviour reminiscent of a minor Royal's stag night.

For the owner, the ideal customer is the one who appreciates the choices, whether food, staff or atmosphere, and who becomes part of the regular clientele.

From each perspective there is the opportunity to observe humans at play, performing a domestic rite, a family experience with observers.

Entering the restaurant for the first time can be an experience full of mixed feelings. You arrive, feel the door handle, hear the sounds of conversation and restaurant clatter, notice the expression of those who greet you, smell the hot food and alcohol. You enter, you are lit and people turn as your entrance is made. Diners examine your dress, your looks, your posture.

Once seated, the awkwardness should diminish. Menus appear, a drink order is taken, bread arrives; drinks follow and the food order is taken. Shoulders drop, jaw muscles relax and the chair begins to feel more comfortable. The first encounter between customer and staff is one that could almost be choreographed. The timing and positions are key elements, allowing the customer time to adapt and relax after the initial stressful moments of arrival. The host gets the newcomers to the right table efficiently, ensuring that menus and something to eat happen immediately. Then he allows a pause to let the mood and ambience develop before the order is taken. It may seem long to an anxious waiter but essential for the good mood of the table. From then on it is a question of sensing what the table needs. Speedy efficiency with the minimum of attention or a slower pace with information flowing on food preparation or the merits of the wine list.

While the restaurateur can develop a perception which

allows for instant appraisals, the customer will sense the restaurant from those initial actions. Successful restaurateurs use their senses unconsciously. The way someone arrives and their gestures, looks, composure and body movements, all present a picture to the observant host.

The busy successful dining room has a formidable atmosphere: robust, infectious and fun, with a momentum all of its own. There is a buzz in the air, the kitchen flows, the waiters glide, the manager is everywhere: laughter, the clink of glasses, movement and mixed aromas —all belong and contribute.

The interactions between staff and guests, the awareness of customer needs, the owner's motivation of the restaurant team — these are the factors which make for success. Sensitivity may be the key attribute for the restaurant owner, for restaurants are not simply places to eat in, they provide feasts for the senses.

CHAPTER SIX

BAR OPERATIONS

With the change in licensing laws, a more relaxed attitude has developed to restaurant licensing. Alcohol can now be sold from 11 am to 11 pm and, with extensions, even later. Few operations can survive without the sale of liquor, except for lower-priced, fast turnover operations such as coffee shops, sandwich bars and cafes.

It is far simpler to produce a beverage item for customers than the dish on the menu, and cheaper. With an average beverage cost factor of 35 per cent there is less to deduct from the gross profit in terms of ancillary costs such as labour, fuel and equipment. The profit margin is greater for liquor sales than food.

The addition of a bar into the restaurant operation may cause problems as well as increased profits: licensing applications; drunks; costly stocks to maintain and guard; the indulgence of employees — there is a distinct loss of innocence as the first cases of drink are wheeled in and a perceptive change in atmosphere as glasses clink and corks pop.

Allowing the passing public to glimpse scenes of a bar crowd enjoying a few drinks can be a great draw for the restaurant. Most bars are kept secluded from public gaze, only revealing glimpses through an opening door or shapes behind frosted glass. There are few bars with floor-to-ceiling windows allowing total exposure to the street. This may be a throwback to the days when there was guilt in enjoying a few drinks and, despite the recent liberation of customers from prehistoric controls of when and where they may enjoy a drink, there still prevails a certain tradition when it comes to public drinking.

The style of each operation can be assessed from the view outside, by looking at the frontage and whatever hint is given about the interior atmosphere. Just how much is visible from the outside depends on whether the restaurant is conveying discretion or bravura.

There are bars which happen to serve food, and restaurants which serve drinks, and until recently the emphasis has been on one activity or the other. The market has been truly segmented into drinkers and eaters, and in establishments which serve both without restrictions one aspect has usually suffered — the drinker has been unable to enjoy a glass of wine in a favourite restaurant without a proper meal, or to eat supper in a pub which only serves food at lunch-times.

Eventually there will be a unity within eating and drinking establishments and one activity will not preclude the other. It seems nonsensical to open a restaurant with a bar and not be able to serve someone a drink without an order for food. Only a full liquor licence permits this, and obtaining a full liquor licence is still a problem, coping with objections from other establishments being one of the major hurdles.

Of all the operations in the restaurant the bar requires most vigilance. Alcohol, cash, telephones and paperwork are all found at the bar and the barman has to be a trusted member of the team as well as becoming a recognised personality.

Before the bar becomes operational a system for storing and issuing the bar products must be established. The decision to stock a wide variety of drinks will mean a high capital outlay and this choice will be determined by the importance of potential bar business and the space available both at the bar and in storage areas. The other consideration is whether the bar will be used simply to dispense drinks to the waiters for service at table, or whether there will be seating at the bar with stools and/or tables and chairs separate from the dining area.

Whatever emphasis is given to the bar stock, the important thing is the display and presentation of what is available and the means to serve drinks at the right temperature in the appropriate glass.

Setting up a bar for the first time requires experience in serving a variety of drinks, from mixing cocktails to drawing a pint of draught beer. The novice should certainly visit several establishments to get an idea of how bars function in restaurants and the sort of equipment used — better still, go and work in one. And if the management has no experience of bar operations it might be worth hiring some expertise in order to train and establish an efficient system.

A bar area with its own seating is especially useful when a single diner turns up. Selling a table to a single means the loss of one potential cover for that particular period. By seating the customer at the bar the loss is avoided and the customer has a least a bartender for company rather than reminding other diners that there is a seemingly lost soul in the room without a partner. The single diner can be a sensitive issue for the restaurant's atmosphere as well as its turnover.

The other advantage of seating capacity at the bar is the ability to put customers there for coffee and liqueurs after a meal is finished thus freeing their table for the next occupants; it is also useful if customers have to wait when a table is not ready.

A different atmosphere may be called for in the bar, one which is comfortable and easy for drinking but which fits into the overall design of the establishment. However, beware the noisy bar which overshadows the dining room. Smoking can also be a problem, and the crowd that simply comes to drink, which can be off-putting for diners.

Behind the bar stands the control for the front-of-house operation. Not only does a bartender mix drinks and give change, there are stocks to check, phones to answer, lights to dim, people to greet. There is the flow of money to control which requires a degree of familiarity with computerised tills, and on top of all these essentials the barman must have a suitable personality. This counts most in developing a good bar trade. The good barman offers a mixture of sophistication and earthiness, an almost unpredictable nature, a fund of good jokes, plus the ability to listen.

A bar following occurs when there is a personality, one which encourages drinkers as well as making the correct welcome for diners. The bartender controls the mix of the crowd at the bar by encouraging some and discouraging others, creating the eventual combination of people for the establishment. Crowd-mixing is an art.

The bar becomes the filter for the dining room — problem customers can be spotted, known regulars dealt with in a familiar way. Usually the bartender is the first member of staff to encounter the customer and those first impressions can colour the whole experience. Bartenders must make instant appraisals, anticipate troublemakers, and understand and control the functions of the restaurant. They must appreciate alcohol as opposed to being professional drinkers. They must know when to offer a free drink and when to warn the manager about possible trouble.

Encouragement of a following is essential for good relations. The bartender can develop this if he is able to attract other local retailers in the area such as the hairdresser, the florist, the antique dealer, the owner of the corner shop. These people can be instrumental in the success of the neighbourhood restaurant and bar and they can be cultivated. Remembering an anniversary or an invitation for a drink establishes the bartender as someone who, like the owner, is able to entertain and promote the establishment.

The bartender should cultivate such patrons and encourage them to enjoy his company as well as the comfort of the bar. If he manages to convince them of his sincerity, and discuss their problems while avoiding his own, he might gain a sympathetic crowd which becomes the nucleus of your bar trade.

Bars are really shop-front psychiatrists under a different guise — they allow for the exchange of views and the analysis of mutually shared problems. A bartender is often treated as a combination of confessor and analyst, dispensing advice along with alcohol — the spiritual therapist.

BAR MANAGEMENT

Stocking up Before each session the bar should be checked. Fresh supplies are drawn from the cellar or storage area which will invariably be a lock-up facility, and these stocks must be recorded.

The simplest form of stock record is the bin card system whereby every item has a card with the product name, the supplier, and two columns, one for stock entries and one for withdrawals, plus space for dates and signatures. Another method is to write up a list of items taken from stock on the check basis and every week the checks are written up in the master ledger for purchases and sales. Draught beers, lagers and ciders will require special handling and gas cylinders and cooling facilities. The installation and servicing can be done by the supplier, usually a brewery.

Stocking up can also require a rotation of supplies in order to sell the oldest items first. Where there are cooling facilities at the bar for cold drinks this must be taken into account because certain beverages, especially carbonated drinks and white wines, can deteriorate after being stored at low temperatures.

When stocking up a bar, the bottles on display must be checked for cleanliness and all the shelves and cabinets cleaned thoroughly on a regular basis along with beer pipes and refrigerators.

Equipment One of the problems for bars offering a full range of drinks concerns the choice of glasses. Beware of the temptation to use a different glass for each type of drink: the space required for a range of glasses would be impossible in a small establishment. The minimum requirements are an all-purpose glass for spirits and cocktails, a wine glass and a beer or water glass. Remember though, that accustomed drinkers do expect the appropriate glass for their favourite beverage. There are certain benefits in choosing machine-made crystal glassware which, although finer than the cheaper non-crystal variety, has a longer life; the brandy balloon and the champagne flute should be of sufficient quality to reflect the necessary standards.

Perhaps the major consideration is the cost of replacements, glassware being the most frequent casualty of careless handling or inadequate storage space.

Other equipment to think about in the bar area includes bottle openers, cork-screws, knives, cutting boards for fruit, cocktail shakers, ice-storage utensils, jugs for water and juices, plus the equipment needed for any food service at the bar including hot beverages such as coffee and tea.

In a busy bar the supply of ice is critical. An ice machine is essential for any restaurant which aims for an established bar business and is generally sited away from the bar. However, there is an absolute need for ice storage at the bar and the best method in a limited space is the triple sink unit. One sink is used for washing, the second for rinsing and the third for ice storage, the advantage of the drain being obvious.

In a fully functional bar it will be necessary to wash,

rinse and dry glasware. This can be done most easily with the use of a special glass-washing machine which brings the temperature of the wash cycle to the required 77°C (170°F). Otherwise some heating unit will be necessary, or chemicals to sterilise the glasses.

In addition to the space required for bottle and glass storage, for ice and other supplies at the bar, space is also needed to store empty bottles and rubbish. The limited space available can accommodate all these functions by proper planning and clever design. Only through experience can a bar designer maximise the use of the space available.

House brands In busy bars there is often a supply of house brands for the most popular spirits and mixed drinks. A gin and tonic or a Scotch and ginger need not necessarily mean using proprietary brands when a cheaper one is available. Pouring spirits are used as opposed to the leading names for each category. New York establishments with busy bars often use speed racks. These are racks located under the bar top which store the house brands used for such drinks as Scotch, vodka and gin, topped with pourers for faster flow and used in mixed drinks or cocktails.

Measures in licensed premises must conform to the legal standard. Spirits, for example, are sold in measures of a quarter, one-fifth or one-sixth of a gill using either a standard container or optic, providing this conforms to the new approved style. And, undoubtedly, legislation will soon come to bring in a standard measure for wine sold by the glass.

Calculation of liquor costs can be more precise than food because of the common sizes and capacities in supplies. A normal size bottle of spirits, 75 cl, yields at least 24 single measures. A bottle of gin costing £6.00 means a unit cost of 25p, and the average charge for a measure of gin is somewhere in the region of £1.00, showing an approximate gross profit of 75 per cent; the cost of ice and garnish will have a minimal effect on the unit cost.

Suppliers The normal sources of supply for the bar are the major brewing companies and independent wholesalers of wines, spirits and beers. Most of these companies sell a variety of items but specialise in one aspect. It is essential to shop around as there is healthy competition, especially in the supply of beers and spirits.

Try to find a local supplier if only for ease of deliveries, especially when it comes to wines. Certain wine suppliers will store wine at the warehouse once it is bought and will deliver small amounts when required. The ease of returning stock is a factor to consider.

Buying spirits is far simpler than buying wines; there are brands which will always be needed and it is easy to compare prices. With wine there are so many different companies to choose from; recommendations are needed to get the two or three major suppliers who will make up most of the list, and some firms will print lists for you.

Suppliers also have stocks of bar equipment and accessories, usually in the form of promotional materials, which may become collectors' pieces eventually.

There are varying discounts offered by drink suppliers, and the price for a regular supply of house wines, for example, can fall significantly if a sufficient quantity is ordered.

WINES

Buying wine for investment can be one of the advantages of becoming a restaurateur, providing there is sufficient storage space. It can be worthwhile to invest in some excellent recent vintages to sell in a couple of years, or to lay down for a longer and perhaps personal benefit.

The ability to buy and sell wine is the most satisfying aspect of holding a licence. Many restaurants start with their owners having specialised knowledge in either food or wine but rarely both; one or the other subject is learned along the way. Wine knowledge is a vast subject, possibly the most complex in terms of planning and operating a restaurant.

The choice of wines reflects the seriousness of the owner in establishing a reputation for fine wines, as well as having relevance to the food. The length of the list will depend on storage space. As with the menu, start with a small list and get wise counsel from a reputable source. Perhaps the best way for the novice is to use a consultant or wine writer. Their current information about recent vintages and sources of supply can provide a wealth of knowledge which has been gleaned from numerous tastings and exchanging information with other experts. Wine consultants usually act as freelances and are not beholden to any one shipper or producer. They will have favourites of course, but they provide a useful short cut to the right suppliers for a consistent source.

The safe wine list contains the usual cliches; the adventurous aims for a different approach giving a variety of lesser-known wines, equivalent to some of the familiar brand leaders but cheaper and tasting even better. The introduction of new wines to the customer has become far easier with the amount of exposure the wine trade has on television and in the press, and as a result there is more desire to experiment with unusual wines from different areas of the world.

The supplier is the most important element in achieving better wine sales. A reputable supplier will recommend other suppliers to fill the gaps that his own company can't supply, provide training sessions for waiters, hold cases at the warehouse, and provide reasonable credit arrangements. Most suppliers hold tastings; good companies will give a tasting specifically for your new project and in order to do so will want to try the food the restaurant intends to put on the menu.

An important choice on the list is the house wine. Very often the cheapest items available are chosen and yet they are supposed to represent the owner's taste not his pocket. The house choice does not have to be the cheapest wine; a better quality can enhance the reputation of the list and allow a wider range of wines to be offered. Aim for flexibility when starting out; a printed list is costly to change and crossing out the wines no longer available creates the wrong impression.

Skilled service of wine calls for care and respect — it must be stored at the right temperature, handled properly, presented and opened with experience, and the correct amount poured into an appropriate glass. It sounds obvious and simple, yet so many establishments get it wrong. To get a good idea of what a proper wine service entails, visit a good hotel restaurant where there is a long list and specialist wine waiters. Watch how they present the bottle to the host. Observe the technique of using the only efficient cork-screw in the business, the 'waiter's friend', of cutting the foil and removing the cork without disturbing the contents or leaving bits; the method of pouring and twisting the bottle upwards to eliminate spillage; placing the wine in a cooler or on the table; replenishing calmly rather than a desperate filling of each glass to the brim every few minutes.

The experienced wine waiter respects the product and knows what it tastes like. Only with constant tastings and discussion can the list be fully appreciated by those who sell it. Remember, the waiting staff should be taught to enjoy wines and to appreciate why a certain wine should be chosen, even if they don't happen to like that particular taste.

Familiarisation with wine service techniques pays

dividends if consistent and correct procedures are followed. Wine lovers who come to a restaurant will pay more attention to everything concerning the wine list and its service than to the menu, and their approval of the wine service can influence a whole new source of business.

Reputations for fine wines develop slowly but add greatly to the stature of any food establishment. Business entertaining often focuses on the wine list; reviewers from the press pay equal attention to originality, and wine buffs love to gossip about an interesting newcomer.

Increasing public awareness about wines means that the potential restaurateur must seriously study the subject. The owner is expected to have an in-depth knowledge when extolling the merits of the list. Reading and tasting, wine seminars and lectures will provide instant help, your suppliers can assist with information and promotional material, and your wine consultant will give specific advice for your operation.

Ultimately, only the experience of drinking wine with food in other restaurants can build up a knowledge of the likes and dislikes of wines. Tastes change and broaden through constant exposure to a variety of wines and their degree of sweetness or dryness.

If personal taste dominates a wine list it will severely restrict its appeal, while a respect for a wide variety of tastes will result in a list with something for everyone. This does not mean that the list should contain a bland mixture of inoffensive items, but it must be recognised that certain wines are popular at every level of sophistication and these tastes should be accounted for.

There can be nothing more satisfying for the restaurateur than to recommend a certain wine and to receive an enthusiastic response, especially when the wine is unknown and a bargain. The operator who plays safe, copying the competition and filling the list with old familiars will never derive that pleasure.

As your wine knowledge increases, the list may expand. Certain restaurateurs develop vast cellars, investing in good current vintages with a view to laying these down and reaping a great profit later. Others begin to display their knowledge by holding wine tastings, organising special dinners around certain types of wine, or even mailing their regular customers with recent acquisitions to the wine list. However serious or frivolous the owner becomes about wines, maintaining a constant source of consistent wines is critical to the restaurant if it aims to be taken seriously and judged accordingly.

With the decisions taken about the content of the wine list and the range of other drinks available at the bar, the beverage service is almost complete. Only the choice of soft drinks and hot beverages remain, and with the increasing amount of non-alcoholic drinks in demand, special attention should be paid to this.

Think about the variety of mineral waters available now. Must the restaurant stock the most popular brand leader or will an alternative suffice? There are sound reasons for selling a wide variety of soft drinks, if only to take account of the stringent drink and drive legislation now in effect.

Another decision affects the choice of juices: freshly squeezed fruit juices remind the customer that there is an authentic approach and using only organic produce enhances this position. In 1980 I opened a restaurant in Greenwich Village, New York. It specialised in wild game, fresh fish and organic produce; the desserts were without white flour or refined sugars. The wine list was simple with only eight choices split equally between whites and reds, plus two champagnes.

Equally important for this list was the attention paid to fruit and vegetable juices, mineral waters, teas and coffees. There were at least five different types of coffee, ranging from a powerful combination of French-roast

Colombian and Italian espresso for a house blend, to a mild decaffeinated Kenya blend, all served in individual glass cafetières. The same importance was given to teas: Lapsang Souchong to Yerba Maté with Keemun and Darjeeling between, and jasmine, mint and chamomile herbal teas were also on offer. We did tastings to compare organic and non-organic raw materials and discovered that organic carrots, for example, produced a much more powerful flavour, not to mention the texture which was altogether more substantial.

Needless to say the operation was ahead of its time, although *Vogue* magazine devoted many column inches to singing its praises. The interesting aspects of the operation were the ability to attract attention for our sources of supply and the original approach of using organic produce and appealing to the healthy-eating minority of the time. Ten years later, this approach is becoming the norm: the current awareness that what happens to our bodies is governed by what we eat and drink requires a greater choice of healthy beverages in addition to wines, beers and spirits.

CHAPTER SEVEN

SALES AND MARKETING

Once the style of restaurant has been chosen, selling it begins. The choice is determined by market research, discovering what potential there is for the product and its price, and consideration of the gaps in the food and drink business within the area selected.

The potential restaurateur has a certain style of operation in mind, illustrated by the first draft of the menu. The location chosen will reflect this, and then the research begins to see if there are comparable operations in the area, to find out where the popular drinking establishments are and to compare their prices and to examine the local environment and any potential business and tourist sources.

The choice of location ultimately determines the style of operation, and if this means a dramatic change in the original concept then the projection will be inaccurate. The style affects the hours of opening, the cost of product, labour and overheads, as well as the average spend. Effective market research is the only way to get the concept on the right track in the potential premises.

As the work begins, the news starts to spread that a new restaurant will be opening. Announcing this means not only that the locals become aware of something new arriving, but also it helps to alert the builders that by a certain date there will be an opening.

Publishing the menu in advance will give a better idea to the passer-by, and the build-up of information about the prospective establishment is achieved by constantly mentioning the project to all the specialists encountered on the way through planning and building, and in local conversations. It is essential to have printed material ready in advance, a card will suffice, but the restaurant must almost exist, albeit in graphic terms, before the actual completion.

The most important aspect of selling the restaurant is the art of getting the right people in and then having them persuade others to come. The best publicity medium is the mouth of a satisfied diner.

The level of sophistication of the restaurant will affect the form of selling. If price is the main consideration, along with speed of service, then a more direct approach is called for: advertising, colourful promotions and special features planned on the menu such as cheap breakfasts or kids' food. When competition is based on price, these features must be well advertised both in the media and at the location. With a more sophisticated style, where price is not so much the consideration and the food and ambience are the feature, the job of selling becomes proportionally more subtle.

Every restaurant must establish a policy on selling. The owner must accept that selling is essential for any restaurant, no matter what its style, and a budget must be allotted for this. The assumption by certain erstwhile operators that simply serving good food and expensive wines will bring the crowds rushing in is illustrated by the high frequency of failures in the business by first-timers within one year of operation. Lack of research, an overconfidence in culinary skills and a disregard for the importance of marketing techniques are often the causes of failure.

In a society which regards the salesman as a lower breed of animal, a belief in the effectiveness of salesmanship is still not fully shared by all who are setting up a business for the first time. Selling the establishment in the appropriate way is only effective when there is a wholehearted commitment to the project and a belief in the powers of selling.

The use of the term marketing, when really the steps described are the true definition of selling, indicates the snobbery that exists. Marketing means the whole process of establishing a business in the market place, and selling is only one aspect of the so-called marketing mix. But selling is the reality of attracting business and should be recognised for the skills in psychology and perception that it requires. Selling is a professional art which deserves more respect.

This is an important message to get across, to the front-of-house staff especially. The waiter, the bartender and the manager are all salesmen. They have to know this: realising the importance of the whole presentation gains the best order and the desire of the customer to return and enjoy the experience again and to recommend it to friends.

There are two aspects of restaurant selling, external and internal: persuading people in the first place to visit, and then selling within the restaurant, which gives the customer pleasure and the owner profit.

EXTERNAL SALES

The hardest part in selling the restaurant is to describe its special quality — the Unique Selling Point (USP), in other words the gimmick. Do not be fooled by sophisticated advice from fly-by-night consultants and smooth-talking public relations types; every business needs something to hang its hat on. The hook in the record business serves a good example, though the restaurant's gimmick should be of a longer lasting quality.

The use of the word gimmick does not demean its importance. The gimmick, or the USP, is what the sales message is built upon and eventually becomes the signpost for recognising a particular establishment. It can be as simple as French fries or as complex as the atmosphere of Le Caprice. Consider well-known and successful restaurants and discover the features that provide their uniqueness. Then think of the lesser-known which are bland, copying here and there, appealing to some ill defined middle-range nowhere land. In an area devoid of good establishments, the cooking alone becomes the USP; where there is more competition something extra needs to be added to gain attention.

A good example of a restaurateur who knew exactly how to produce that something extra was Charles Chevillot of La Petite Ferme in New York, where I worked during my early years in the business.

La Petite Ferme was in the village, Greenwich Village, Manhattan. It was a tiny jewel of a place and its rustic, farmyard look fitted in with the post-bohemian feel of the area. There was one of those half curtains across the window, a stable door, an awning and a flower box, and inside seven small tables of different sizes in solid wood, with rush-seated chairs. Farm implements hung on the wall and two doves in a cage completed the pastoral atmosphere.

The menu was short and every item on it was fresh and bought daily. The specialities were French bourgeois, regional cooking from Burgundy with adaptations for the American sources of supply.

Charles Chevillot, the owner, was an outstanding restaurateur. He had great style and he was a perfectionist who loved good food and fine, classic wines.

Charles was a social being; he entertained often and cultivated highly influential contacts in the world of fashion, the lifeblood of the New York social scene. Givenchy and Bill Blass, Geoffrey Beene and Oscar de la Renta all appeared regularly.

This exclusivity was established with help from good connections in the public relations business and a good lineage from Europe, plus the wily input from Charles who created the illusion of constant success and a full restaurant.

The rumours put it about that a table was not to be had for at least three weeks, and so demand grew. New York is like that.

This was Charles with a typical telephone call in the early years: 'A table for two? Tonight?', his voice slightly incredulous and very French.

'I'm sorry, we're completely full. Tomorrow?' More incredulity. 'No, I'm sorry, there's nothing available. I could do something next Monday at 7.30. Yes? Right, and the name please.'

In fact, the reservation book for that particular evening was virtually empty. It was 11.30 in the morning and Charles would never accept twos first thing. If a party of four had telephoned, then the reaction may have been different. To Charles it was more important to create this reputation of being impossible to get a table than to sell two covers at any cost.

The policy worked, because the place was small, and the beautiful people needed to add something new to their repertoire. And Charles was aiming at the right target.

The interesting bit about the whole procedure was that he never asked for the name first. He did not care who it was. The important thing was to put across the image of a complete success.

Creating the selling point, what ever it is, focuses the attention on precisely what the restaurant's appeal is to the relevant market and provides the basis for eventual sales promotions, graphics and publicity.

With a simple menu featuring one type of speciality, a theme is often used to provide the setting and presentation which will put the product in an eye-catching manner, one that is easily remembered. At the other extreme, a discreet name meaning nothing and with little attention paid to extravagant frontages, gives a subtle impression and relies on informed sources to bring customers throught the door.

The dilemma occurs for the middle-range operation, caught between the reality of needing a high-volume business and the desire to establish a smart watering hole for the rich and famous. There will be a need to advertise, devise suitable sales promotions and employ public relations (PR) techniques. But be careful how you spend money on professional advice: the services of a restaurant public relations firm can come in the form of an individual with a vast appetite for expensive rarities promising pages in Sunday supplements and mentions in the gossip columns.

When setting up for the first time in an area of great competition and high-density population, more cash will have to be put aside for the promotional budget. Away from the conurbations, the owner can arrange more of the publicity using effective public relations techniques.

The main advantage in using a good public relations agency is its contacts with the media, especially with food journalists, reviewers and style columnists. Sound advice can be had from the reputable specialists, but comment on menu content, staffing, decor and promotional budgets can be more forthcoming than useful tips for increasing business. Paying constant monthly retainers, as well as providing all those expensive rarities for a procession of the PR's friends and groupies, must be seen to produce significant results.

Public relations are the means by which the restaurant becomes known to the public that represents the market for its business, and they are achieved by promoting the restaurant through the media and producing promotional schemes to encourage more business. Public relations techniques are generally regarded as the most effective ways of increasing and measuring sales.

Many restaurants at the top end of the scale employ a professional PR service, others perform it themselves. Because the restaurant business has a reputation for gaining business through word of mouth, the editorial piece in the press will have more effect than an advertisement; this is the principal reason why many restaurants do not advertise.

Restaurant advertising tends to be highly specialised; theatre programmes are a favourite choice for late-night operations or those located nearby. Advertisements in local guides for the tourist traffic is another example, but advertisements in the general press appealing to a wide audience are expensive and the results hard to trace.

The clip-out coupon offering a free something seems a dated approach but it will provide an indication of the advertisement's success, and the lack of any customers providing bits of newspaper at the table to qualify for a free glass of mediocre plonk will suggest that the advertising is not paying for itself.

Advertising can be most effectively used by choosing the right medium to announce an opening, to feature a special promotion, or to promote another activity of the restaurant such as private parties, catering or food to take out.

The first piece of written material featuring the restaurant which is not paid for will usually be some form of review. Getting the local press into the restaurant is fairly simple. Food is news, chefs become personalities, and journalists are generally hungry creatures. It is the timing of such an exercise which is critical. The wise owner restrains himself from obtaining any reviews until the shake-down period is complete and the kitchen has a fair chance of producing the menu consistently.

Getting national coverage is more difficult. The serious

daily newspapers have the most clout and most of them employ full-time restaurant reviewers who do not always feature Wandsworth and Soho.

Regional newcomers who have gained some local press often find themselves included in a group of established operations written up in a feature article.

Reviewers love to be the first to discover something new and interesting and the information must come directly from the restaurant unless another source such as the restaurant PR does the job. It is worthwhile contacting all the leading food writers and reviewers when the time is right, and not all at once. Include any previous write-ups, as well as the menu and a brief description of opening times and prices and a photograph.

Successful PR is a planned campaign and does not hit everyone at once with the good news. Selected journalists and editors are approached at different times, each with a different slant on the same story. The medium is the message.

Another good media choice is a mention in the various restaurant guides, especially the four leading ones from the AA, Egon Ronay, the Consumers Association and Michelin (*see page 148* ***Suggested Reading***). The choice in this instance however is theirs, not the restaurateur's. Alert them anyway, sending as much information as soon as it is known, before the place opens. It takes a least a year or more to see if there will be a mention, but a guide listing is a very good source of new business, especially in tourist areas.

Many establishments celebrate the opening with a party, and some make the mistake of inviting as many press as possible. This can produce write-ups perhaps, but the prospect of filling the place in the first week brings only disasters. The opening party should be an extravagant house warming for all those involved with setting it up, friends and neighbours, plus a few influential friends of the investors, and maybe some press who need to be cultivated for a later date. This type of opening will bring in some business which later will bring more, but only within a reasonable time, one that allows for a steady build-up and permits the staff to become familiar with production and service routines.

It sounds crazy but do not serve too much food at an opening. Select a few hot and cold appetisers and make them small enought to swallow in one mouthful. Trying to serve the whole menu to a dining room full of party people will be impossible for the first night. It is better to serve a small representation of the style of food, have menus displayed, clear the room to get as many as possible in at once, and pass food and drink — especially drink.

A busy, happy event needs prompt service with a simple range of goodies on offer, lots of people from a wide range of backgrounds, professions and styles, and staggered invitations. Inviting guests to arrive at different times allows more to come and see and sample, spend some time, and then leave to make room for more. And remember that you can stage more than one opening event. There can be two or three to take into account a larger list, if there is faith in this type of promotion and the budget to make it happen.

With no opening party, the operation starts without fanfare and business is slow or non-existent for the first few days. The opening celebration is either kept to the minimum or held at a later date when everything is completed. The problem of dealing with a rush of business after an opening promotion can be handled more easily this way. The staff are more familiar with their tasks and the locations and there might be less chaos if there has been a longer lead time of quiet trading.

When clients arrive for the first time in a new restaurant the critical antennae are out in full array. Recommended to a new place, the first-time guest will be more inclined to criticise, looking for slow service, amateurism and poorly prepared dishes. Bad news travels more quickly than good; by bringing in as many people as possible during the opening weeks mistakes will happen and get more coverage than any good impressions that may have been formed.

Selling, like training, happens constantly. An awareness of salesmanship will come most easily to the owner — it ensures survival. Restaurant owners should always be alert to the possibility of making a sale; whether it comes through talking to a local retailer and discovering that his daughter is about to marry and there is a need for a catered reception somewhere, or persuading the wine supplier to hold a tasting. This selling is an essential part of the owner's day. Owners must eat and should always use the opportunity of entertaining potential clients and useful contacts.

INTERNAL SALES

While external selling brings the customers to the restaurant, internal selling keeps them happy. The job of selling internally is shared by all the front-of-house staff and sometimes the chef. In high-price operations, which use much fresh produce, there is a particular need for subtle salesmanship; perishable items which are not sold one day may be waste the next. Price, too, has a consideration; the ordering of three courses and not one from a full à la carte menu is more difficult to achieve. The fixed price menu offering a complete range of appetiser, main course and dessert is a popular device for keeping the average food spend right.

There are waiters who can sell anyone anything, and with small menus based on fresh materials this power is sometimes necessary to keep the menu in full supply throughout the session, to avoid running out of one particular dish and to avoid waste. High-powered selling at the table is one way of making the sale, in the same way as others might use the foot-in-the-door technique.

There is a way of becoming a trustworthy source of information to the newly arrived diners. The host identifies himself and a certain closeness of confidence can begin. The description of certain items can be done in such a way as to steer the would be chicken-eater into becoming a pigeon-enthusiast for the night, or the red-blooded fillet lover into suddenly starting an affair with steamed salmon and lobster butter.

This familiarity with customers can produce almost secret confidences, so that a certain dish should not be ordered, whereas the partridge that the waiter had enjoyed for lunch is the best meal he will recommend all week. A less roguish approach should certainly entail accurate descriptions of dishes which can only come through the personal experience of the waiter.

The other fundamental of internal selling is to get a balanced order with the knowledge of timing and presentation. The balance of drink orders for instance, the selling of aperitifs, allowing time for them to work and perhaps stimulate the palate before taking the food order. The immediate service of wine into large glasses can bring an order for a second bottle, and after that it is easy to sell a bit more.

The presentation of certain items can sometimes make the sale, but current restrictions on food display mean that few places have adequate equipment to display food safely at correct temperatures with the proper coverings.

Often the presentation of food and drink at other tables can be just as effective; customers craning to observe other choices can suddenly change their minds when something served nearby looks appealing.

The menu, the most important aspect of the point-of-sale experience, is designed as a sales tool. It will contain a list of everything available from the kitchen, bar and cellar, and presents the information in such a way that is relevant to the price structure and the feel of the place, cleverly highlighting whatever is special, noteworthy, or significant.

Flexibility is needed in the presentation of the menu, especially for the seasonal operation. There are several effective and cheap ways of printing or copying the menu and wine list which can be incorporated into a longer-lasting, substantial format. The cheapest way of producing a menu is the faithful blackboard and chalk, whether it is fixed to a wall or a small portable school-type blackboard and easel.

On the other hand the feel of a printed menu conveys a certain tactile message — the choice of paper or plastic-coated card, for example, says something about the restaurant (durability being another consideration).

Menu language is important for clarity, with the use of familiar terms in the descriptions. In an English speaking country it would seem too obvious to recommend printing menus in clear, well written English. However it does need stating if only to illustrate the number of menus we see with English descriptions of a French dish full of terms which are themselves French — quenelle, mousseline, feuilleté, coulis . . . .

Selling in the restaurant is all about creating memories for the customer. He arrives, is welcomed and eats and drinks well; enjoys the ambience and the other guests; leaves feeling comfortable, recalling highlights of the experience: these are all the objectives of the salesman. The art is making this happen and selling the menu well on behalf of the house.

Good salesmen in the dining room remember names and faces; recall idiosyncracies. Sometimes files are kept to build up client lists and mailing opportunities. Names are gleaned from the reservations book and credit card slips. A visitors book at the opening party would be the starting point; thereafter regulars and big spenders are noted, their preferences in seating, the waiter, and any particular favourite specialities or wines. Anniversaries should be recorded and Christmas bookings remembered.

With selling must come the incentives for the staff. For the owner it is obvious; for the staff on the floor it can be the tip and perhaps points for selling the most wine, or the best sales over a fortnight at lunch or dinner. Beginners can be encouraged by taking them out and showing them superb service in a good restaurant. Then there is profit sharing for the chef and manager.

The art is getting to the people-movers in the first place. Start locally with the hairdresser, the hall porter, the cab driver; they are all good talkers and rely on news for conversation fillers. Become newsworthy. The florist, the estate agent, the antique dealer, all possess information about their particular clients, have frequent access to them, and like to talk.

Everyone the owner knows has a contact with someone who can recommend the restaurant; every member of staff knows someone and can use their position to promote the establishment; and each investor has a useful store of potential clients.

Suppliers can also be productive especially when the contra deal is used, contra dealing being a fancy term for bartering. Take paintings as an example. The owner may have a distinct taste for contemporary art, may know some artists and dealers, or some struggling painters or photographers who are becoming established in their individual fields.

There is an opportunity as an owner of a restaurant to gather art and pay for it in food and drink. Whether the artwork becomes a special feature or simply an integral part of the decor, it can be acquired through bartering, which means that the artist will bring his friends to the restaurant where his art is on the walls and blank spaces are on the bills. There is the trick of getting hold of the right artists and local personalities, who know the potential customers, who have a varied social life, but not those who are the isolated ivory-tower types.

Restaurants become known primarily for the quality of their food and drink, coupled with value for money at different levels of operation. It is the uniqueness which attracts attention to these qualities and it is the consistency which keeps the business flowing.

CHAPTER EIGHT

STAFFING THE RESTAURANT

A successful restaurant must be entertaining. Great food, creatively presented, expertly served in a handsome setting make up the main elements. Lighting, decor and possibly music also contribute part of the atmosphere. But there must be more, and it is the combination of staff and their customers that allows the entertainment to occur. Restaurant staff need to be versatile, good-humoured and strong. The work is demanding. Many restaurant people have an affinity with the theatre; there are similarities in the roles of each: actors, like restaurant staff, form close-knit family groups. Both love to entertain, are sensitive, require inspired direction, motivation and clever incentives. They have to be malleable and be willing to be taught new ways in a short space of time. They are interdependent. Staff must be able to project humour and yet be able to judge moments when they should be serious, whilst always retaining their professional skills.

Choosing people to serve customers is a skill requiring almost clairvoyant judgement. There is an important qualification which applies to front-of-house staff in particular and that is the ability to be accepted by either sex. The ambi-sexual nature of waiters and barmen is both a mysterious and subtle quality. The guest should feel at ease yet somehow be attracted enough to allow the waiter to take control of the meal and to rely on his judgement and recommendations. This quality of attraction, having little to do with sexual inclination, is a natural outcome when the job is enjoyed for what it is, and with the realisation that earnings are directly related to the relationship with the customer.

Look for alertness in staff; restaurants are not strangers to crises. The chef can slice something off a finger, the kitchen porter can break a leg or the barman may need to leave town in a hurry. If the waiter has worked in the kitchen, the commis knows how to operate the dishwashing machine, and the manager can shake a good cocktail, then such a crisis becomes less of a problem and possibly even amusing. This form of training — the swapping of roles — keeps staff on their toes, helps them to learn more skills, and makes them appreciate each other's contributions.

Providing incentives is another way of improving performance, helping to keep staff and increasing sales. Prizes, trips and bonuses are devices which come under this heading and most of them apply to back-of-house staff. Tips are the incentive for front-of-house and they represent sensitive areas of dispute in the restaurant. Kitchen and supporting staff do not usually share in the tip payout. According to waiter lore, tips are an expression of approval, or otherwise, of the standard of service of meal. They have no relation to the preparation, as the customer expects that the kitchen staff are adequately rewarded for their creative labours. Waiters, not being highly paid, rely on tips as part of their earnings. Tips are sacred to them, and woe betide the owner who tries to distribute them. That is the province of the head waiter. The waiter represents the contact between establishment and customer. Furthermore, he is the representative of the owner at the table. The manner of this contact, its development and progress are due solely to the skill of the waiter.

A chef's function is to provide the food for the menu in the best, most consistent way possible. His responsibility is enormous; he is the factory, the producer, the creative force at work. He is always there and is paid on a regular and often very significant basis. But no custom means no tips for the waiter, who gambles on receiving tips as a boost to his low income; the chef is not involved.

It is this contrast between gambles and assured income that forms the background and tension between front- and back-of-house. The waiter's argument about tips and their final resting place maintains that the tip is the reward for the extra care he takes to ensure that the customer enjoys his meal. Quite rightly in my view, the waiter expects the food he serves to be cooked properly and to be well presented on clean equipment. What he does, apart from simply putting it down and then taking away the empty plates, is to give something personal to the table. He allows himself to be cast in a ubiquitous role; he becomes involved in the mood of each table and judges each moment; when to approach, when to clear, with whom to make contact so that the speed of the meal is appropriate to that particular table. These skills are part of the subtleties of professional service and are directly related to tips.

If the waiter is not allowed to control his tips and their distribution, then his service will be one-dimensional and insensitive. Anyone can wait on tables, but a skilled waiter provides service, sympathy and subtlety. Good waiters know about food and drink; they understand the composition of each dish they are selling, and will have tasted them. They are aware of the power they possess to make a meal pleasurable or distressing, and can dramatically affect the income of the restaurant. To ignore this fact, and to treat waiters as mere servants is a mistake freqently made by foolish owners and contemptuous chefs.

Kitchen staff have their hang-ups too, and the obvious one is connected with their creativity. The waiter's skill lies in his personality winning him bigger tips and the chef's in the ability to recreate fine dishes consistently. A chef knows instinctively if what he has cooked is good. The chef's awareness of his art and the self-critical nature of his work means that he rewards himself. Hence, chefs are temperamental. Working behind the dining room door in the privacy of the kitchen, chefs can avoid customer confrontation. The waiter receives the praise or criticism for a dish and, if he knows how to handle his job, lets the kitchen know about success and disaster, keeping the ordinary to himself. The satisfaction for the chef happens when great dishes are produced and he knows it. Like the satisfaction for a painter stepping back from a completed picture admiring the work and respecting the integrity of the craft and imagination, so is the feeling in the kitchen when it produces well.

The art of the chef is the ability to combine skills and techniques with well-developed taste: preparation, timing, speed and accuracy are the essentials of kitchen method, plus an ability to teach others, while seasoning, flavouring and presentation are more natural gifts. There are many who profess to be natural chefs; there are few who can claim mastery in the kitchen and provide consistently good food. That is the test for hiring a chef, after determining whether he can demonstrate knowledge of professional techniques and a talent to season and flavour. The critical test is the ability to produce constant repetitions of the perfect dish. Hollandaise or rare steak au poivre can be performed by most amateurs for the odd Sunday lunch; professionals repeat these masterpieces time after time without the revealing array of amateur variations. Successful restaurants rely on good reviews from critics and regular customers; the kitchen needs to be consistent for the good news to go forth.

The relationship between kitchen and front-of-house is often chilly, based on distrust, envy or paranoia. Chefs can be very difficult, especially during moments of tension at the busiest periods. Impatient with waiters, scornful of their lowly status and deriding their lack of knowledge about the finer points of intricate dishes, chefs can disturb the atmosphere and negatively affect the operation. Yet a chef needs the waiter in order to make his job easier. The waiter is the eyesight of the kitchen, who can report on the state of the dining room, the atmosphere, which tables are 'good', and describe the appearance of the arrivals at the bar. The waiter judges the timing of each table, and can tell the chef if there is likely to be a delay on one or if another requires faster service. It is in the interest of the wise chef, therefore, to stay calm and respect the front-of-house staff. Waiters are in the public domain, and while they represent the management to the customer, they also represent the customer to the kitchen. This is rarely recognised in the kitchen, and the relationship breaks down when demands are made, changes in an order occur or something is sent back. It is the customer making the fuss, not the waiter!

It is the manager's responsibility to avoid poor relations between sections of the staff, and the way to break down the walls of antagonism is to encourage staff to perform each other's work. In this way there can be an appreciation of the peculiarities and difficulties of all roles in the restaurant.

Every business needs a person in charge. Plays need a director, governments a leader and restaurants a manager. Democracy is a wonderful concept but it only works when the elected leader leads. The restaurant manager owes his position to employees accepting his authority, while he retains the ability to listen and use criticism of his performance to improve the overall efficiency.

Restaurants serve food and drink — that is their primary function — and food is the item that reviewers talk about most. It is the manager who ensures that the chef is the star of the production, not upstaged or kept locked behind the kitchen door for ever. This is the most important and underlying role of the manager, to recognise that the food comes first and everything that follows is a support of that principle. The ways in which he achieves this depend upon his personality and the degree to which he can combine informality and a pleasant attitude with a sense of discipline and authority.

The manager is a parent figure to the restaurant family whom both staff and customers recognise as authority and an informed yet benevolent power. The manager's daily routine is split between organising and performing. To fulfil both tasks successfully, the personality required for organisation is very different from that required for performance. To recommend schizoid behaviour patterns would be going too far; nevertheless the first essential is discipline when coping with daily returns, dealing with wily suppliers and organising the preparations for service. But the personality must change as soon as the door is opened for business, from the parent figure to the welcoming host who can charm and exercise diplomacy.

It is the inability to make this change that can cause tensions on the floor. Waiters who are terrified of a tongue-lashing for simply dropping a fork on the floor, and guests witnessing harsh discipline do not make for happy times. A common fault of managers is to correct faults during service, or even to tell the offending waiter to disappear while he takes over. Only the most disastrous mistakes warrant such action, and a mistake can be readily turned into something amusing rather than become a drama and thereby made worse. After a manager has seated the table and taken the order, the waiter takes over. The manager only intervenes at the beginning and possibly at the end. This is a natural approach and allows for an unfussy service. Confusion reigns when the manager comes to the table and asks the same question already covered by the waiter. Confused ordering and duplicate service is a screeching example of amateurism in would-be wonderful restaurants.

It is surely a treat when service is anticipatory as a result of attentive waiters. But the eating experience palls when managers intrude too much; fussy, over-attentive service creates a poor memory. A slower, more controlled meal, where each member of the hierarchy performs his own task expertly, is much pleasanter.

When a manager is responsible for profitability, he can be a nagging element in the mix rather than the detached, controlling influence. Of course, tables must be turned over to provide income and service must therefore be efficient. But never forget that the meal experience is the reason for the guest to be there and unless there is obvious value for money in the food itself, the service, and the possibility for the guests to linger and enjoy themselves, ultimately there will be no guests at all. Greedy managers who insist on turning over tables to maximise profit are shortening the life of the restaurant and their own careers.

The manager, like the parent of the growing child, must care that growth is carefully planned, that development is gradual to ensure a firm basis for eventual maturity and health. The rush for money during the first year of the restaurant is understandable. So many operations which depend on the projected income to provide the repayment of loans suffer from being forced into a short burst of growth, only to decline just as quickly when clients are deterred by overcrowding, by being rushed from tables, or by the many other problems that can be traced to the manager who forces too much too soon.

Training employees is the job of the manager, not to turn them out as faithful replicas, but in a way that allows them to express their own individuality while exercising professional techniques. The manager will have worked in all areas of the restaurant — this is essential before he can teach. The respect which a manager receives from staff depends upon his own ability as a waiter, barman, and at least sous-chef.

Other types of business can be run by managers who know little about production skills; restaurant managers need to be experts in all areas of the business. This is one of the most important distinctions that sets restaurants apart in a world of their own. Apart from training, managers must be able to fill in if a member of the restaurant staff doesn't show. In some businesses a gap may not be noticed, but in this service business a missing chef or barman cannot be faked. A restaurant can manage for a time without the manager's presence simply because it relies on the team doing its job. Nothing endears a manager more to the staff, if the dishwasher goes AWOL, than for the person in charge to take a spell at the machine for the session!

Creating a pleasurable experience for the guest takes many forms. The chef makes sublime food, the waiter you may fall in love with, the music and lights are soothing, while the cleanliness and order would satisfy the most stringent inspector. The manager pulls it all together with an eye for detail. This alertness during service and the amount of preparation beforehand means that the responsibility for production is great indeed.

Managing a restaurant is a task which is tiring both mentally and physically. It requires stamina and a great amount of observation.

No-one but the manager sees the restaurant with the same detail from the points of view of both customer and employee.

Perhaps the most fruitful time for the manager is the staff meal. It is here that the day is at its most relaxed. It is the time for analysis, announcements and conviviality. All the staff sit down to sift through previous times, talk about their problems and share in their successes. It is a time when chef, waiter and manager can sit down and chew over whatever needs to be improved or changed. It is a time when new dishes can be tried and grievances aired. The manager must use this occasion for what it is — a relaxed time of the day when all the people involved are together and can participate in making the place human, cohesive and fun.

THE IDEAL RESTAURANT STAFF

- *The bartender* key attribute: empathy.
  A drinker — someone who knows about drinking, not a drunk. Good on initial impressions. Has knowledge of the menu. A crowd pleaser, an extrovert. Speedy and accurate. Honest, good at figures. Organised. Has good telephone manner. A story teller, anecdotal.
- *The waiter* key attribute: efficiency.
  An eater with knowledge of the menu and its preparation. A chameleon, able to adapt his personality from table to table — from business group here, to loving couples there. Has a different face for every table, and a form of sexual/sensual ambiguity: the ability to be attractive to whoever makes the decision. A judge of timing, mood and atmosphere. Shows good balance with agility and fast reactions. Serves others with self respect and a sense of professionalism.
- *The chef* key attribute: consistency.
  Balances artistic flair and kitchen management. A teacher, a paternal authoritarian and a communicator. Recognises the restaurant as an entity, not split into front and back. Respects the serving process, maintains close liaison with the manager and head waiter. Strong, energetic, sober and hygienic. Views food as an art and a science to be enjoyed by everyone.
- *The manager* key attribute: responsibility.
  Demonstrates operational skills with charm and a thorough understanding of food and drink. Has good physical presence, an ability to project self-confidence. A leader, delegating authority not responsibility. Shows respect for record keeping and controls. Retains overall view of the restaurant operation, maintaining harmony with the kitchen and respect for the kitchen team. Is genial with a good memory.

CHAPTER NINE

EXPANDING THE BUSINESS

PRIVATE CATERING

This is a development which can naturally emerge as business increases. It is well worth considering this as part of the future expansion when setting up, especially when planning the kitchen and service equipment. There can be a significant income from catering, whether for private parties in the restaurant or larger events outside. Owning a restaurant brings with it the facility of providing food and drink for large numbers on or off the premises, and it makes financial sense not to under-use such a prime asset.

As a restaurant becomes known for its quality of food, the more likelihood there is of being asked to cater for special events; there can even be a separate company established to handle a large demand. It is certainly easy to promote the restaurant as a catering organisation. Tent cards on the tables advertising the service can be a start. Easier profits are made in catering: knowing numbers in advance ensures more accurate food costing, with little waste. Large parties mean greater purchasing discounts and often lead to even better prices.

Reputations spread very quickly after a successful event. It is always possible to undertake large parties: extra staff can be booked through agencies in emergencies, but better through personal contacts from the existing staff; equipment can be hired and trucks rented; whole mobile kitchens can be hired for 24 hours with the capacity of producing meals for up to 1,000. There are plenty of supplementary services and contractors available.

Catering is big business. The competition is fierce, but the business can start at a local level. If there is a definite policy in the restaurant to encourage catering then the extra income generated will demonstrate the wisdom of working a little harder for a potentially larger proportion of profit.

With a restaurant site on more than one level, the extra floor can be used for parties. There is an obvious advantage to having the dining room and kitchen on one level, preferably the ground floor, but if necessary the kitchen can be sacrificed to allow the dining room to be on the ground floor level, whilst a floor above can be used for parties. In busy city locations there is always a need for meeting rooms, business entertaining away from the office, or simply social occasions, and a restaurant with space can provide this.

Rural operations with some outside space have the advantage of using marquees or tented extensions to the dining room, and of course the restaurant with no extra space can still use other locations. There should be few occasions which have to be turned down. Size or distance need not be a problem; the availability of cooking staff can be handled with clever timing and by bringing in adequate part-timers for the laborious preparation work.

To gain a reputation as a caterer, the originality and flair must be in evidence: parties are one-off experiences, you only have one shot. Presentation must be in evidence on a grander scale than that needed for the intimacy of the dining room. Certain types of parties call for showmanship and ideally all the details should be coordinated by one individual. If the host is inexperienced then this job often falls to the caterer and, by controlling all the elements which go to make up a party, the caterer has a better chance of success.

Planning of parties is easy providing there is a formula approach, and this is best done by working from an order form. By including all the details on one form ordering is made simple, the number of staff required can be seen, and the equipment can be organised from the same sheet. This can also be used for producing the invoice, and in this way it is kept separate from the main transactions of the restaurant.

Creating memorable parties can be difficult when the host insists on the same tired formula which means black-and-white service, lots of cold poached salmon or hot canapés, all with the same brown tinge. There is not enough imagination in many of the large catering companies to allow for unusually attired waiters, or to display different cooking or original forms of presentation. Parties provide an opportunity, at all levels of style and price, to devise something unusual, especially when there is a reason for celebrating an event or impressing some potential customers at a business presentation.

Parties should be fun and they nearly always are for the staff, providing there are personalities amongst the waiters and hosts who enjoy entertaining. The caterer can provide amusement by bringing in the appropriately extrovert help and by providing celebratory food presented in unusual forms. The caterer's task is made easier if the host can be persuaded to stray from the familiar.

Perhaps the easiest way of illustrating unusual approaches is to give descriptions of a few parties I have been involved in creating.

A cocktail party without canapés

This was a rather grand affair, but the concept works at any level. Instead of penguin look-alikes flat-footing it around the room occasionally with trays full of canapés which last seconds once the vultures swoop, we did something else. We installed ten different small stations, or tables, at strategic areas in the large hallway of a New York town house. Behind each was a cook and a waiter, the chefs in whites, the waiters in different coloured waistcoats, bow ties and long aprons. Food was prepared in front of the 200 guests and then placed on serving platters. Each station had a different theme: there was a sushi chef with a kimono-clad assistant; another had a chef cooking blinis using copper bowls, blini pans, flambé lamp and offering self-service from oversized dishes of smoked salmon and caviar. At another station someone sliced whole, rare, hot fillets of beef onto slices of warm toast with rosemary- and shallot-flavoured butter. In another corner a giant of a fisherman was shucking clams and prising open oysters with ease.

All the stations were serviced by waiters from the kitchen bringing fresh supplies without being mobbed on the way. Drinks were dispensed from two bars at each end of the hall with additional service direct from the kitchen. This method of food and drinks service helped people to circulate. So often activity centres on a bar with waiters floating round the edges of the throng, which means the same people keep being offered the food and drink as it arrives. By creating different food bars the situation was reversed, there was interest everywhere and the crowd was dispersed evenly with lots of intermingling.

A wedding buffet without tables draped in white

This was a large wedding party in the height of summer. We wanted to avoid the cinema queue syndrome which is so often the feature of cold buffets — the long tables with attacked salmon wilting under the canvas, chaud-froid chickens becoming lethal as the aspic warms, overfilled Pavlovas tilting and collapsing as the cream eats into the meringue, rare and tough cuts of beef greying into the afternoon.

Fig 17

THE PARTY ORDER FORM

Client's name.. No. of staff........................ Tim

Address.. Names

....

....

Tel. no. Office..

Home..

Date of party..

No. of guests..

Type of party..

Time to start..

MENU Item	Quantity	Garnish

BEVERAGES & WINES..

....

SUNDRIES Ice............Napkins............Garnish............Doilies............Aprons............Bu

Menus.........Milk.........Cream.........Sugar.........Condiments.........Piping bag.........Knives...

Kitchen equipment..

....

DATE OF ORDER……………………………

RENTAL EQUIPMENT Delivered to……………………………

By……………………………

Item	Quantity	Size or description
Main plate		
Side plate		
Dessert plate		
Saucer – large		
Saucer – small		
Cup – tea		
Demitasse		
Soup plate		
Wine glass		
Champagne tulip		
Tumbler		
Whisky glass		
Knife & fork		
Spoon – dessert & fork		
Spoon – tea		
Spoon – serving		
Cheese knife		
Cruets		
Coffee services		
Ice bucket		
Round trays		
Ashtrays		
Other items		
Linen cloths		
Linen napkins		
Tables		
Chairs		

Confirmed…………………… Date……………………

Deposit……………………………

Food price per head……………………………

Staff cost……………………………

Equipment cost……………………………

Beverage cost……………………………

We came up with the idea of a French country picnic lots of wooden platters and serving wenches, small round tents with flowers climbing up the supporting poles and no side flaps, all arranged around the edge of the lawn with a central tent for the wedding cake. Our oyster opener was in one tent, this time with assistants, cracking crab claws, tossing mussels in red onion, parsley and vinaigrette; there was another group serving an assortment of pâtés with French bread; in another tent whole sides of smoked salmon and crusty loaves of rye and pumpernickel were sliced to order. The guests chose their salads from great wooden bowls of individual ingredients. There was one tent with a barbecue for seafood with prawns, bass wrapped in fennel, and sardines, and another with a barbecue for cooking veal sausages, chicken, or lamb chops marinated in olive oil and provençale herbs.

Guests wandered around dressed up to the nines and enjoyed the almost medieval atmosphere — it only needed Lancelot and Guinevere to complete the scene. The staff looked rustic without that corny amateur-night-at-the-opera look; long aprons, some leather, and denim with a few ruffled shirts, and flowers in the girls' hair. Each tent had its own different coloured striped top with pennants flying. There were wooden tables with bench seating here and there and some more comfortable chairs closer to the main house. The rain alternative meant that a spare tent was available throughout the day, attached to the main house.

Old barrels were filled with ice for the champagne and these were the focal points of three bars, treated in the same manner as the food areas. More barrels were used for rubbish and bottles. There was not one silver-plated tray or candelabrum for miles, not a white cloth in sight, and no salmon heads leering at the guests from black plastic bin liners.

A party picnic

Sometimes a miniature picnic hamper can be put to good effect. A party was held in a rambling flat on two levels with small rooms all over the place, and a minuscule kitchen where a cat would survive only a quarter of the swing. Hot food was out of the question. With no real space for a buffet table and trolleys unusable because of the stairs, the solution was to give everyone a miniature picnic hamper.

In those days fresh mushrooms were sold in 2-lb punnets: wafer-thin, wooden, oblong baskets, they were the perfect size for a hamper. We provided an assortment of goodies: cold chicken Kiev wrapped in foil; two potatoes of the small, new variety, scooped out and filled with sour cream and topped with salmon and caviar, and placed on a bed of watercress in a flat, translucent plastic box with a separate clear lid. Four peeled prawns with a cherry tomato filled with garlic mayonnaise; a small tub of asparagus and bean salad; another of pasta salad with basil and pine nuts completed the main course. Cold lemon soufflé in a paper cup garnished with strawberries were to follow, some sugar-dipped grapes and chocolate-covered orange slices, again in those plastic boxes with views, and airline-size bottles of wine and mineral water.

We assembled the hampers at the last minute, and travelled about as best we could dispensing wines, coffee and more food from larger baskets. Everyone was sitting around, perched on stairs, leaning against the piano or hanging over the fire escape. They all had their mushroom baskets lined with paper napkins, complete with glass, cutlery and cruet sachets. And in every basket was a bookmatch with the company name and logo, complete with telephone number and address.

Most of the guests and the hosts were young lawyers from two or three big, city firms, and many of them were single and contemplating marriage. That party led to at least another dozen or so good-sized parties, many of them wedding receptions, on the strength of the originality of the picnic idea.

TAKE-AWAY

The take-away business is another way of expanding without extra installations or hiring additional staff, and take-away food implies that catering is part of the restaurant's operation. Smart, sensible packaging is essential, achieved quite simply using standard boxes and cartons and adding a self-adhesive label with your logo and telephone number.

A separate menu may develop as the take-away side of the business increases and tent cards in the restaurant can draw attention to this service. Providing a tray of cold appetisers to a local business for an in-house meeting could lead to a regular supply and on to proper lunches or parties later.

Providing a take-away service boosts the turnover of food which can bring greater purchasing discounts and, at the same time, act as an advertisement for quality and presentation. Think of the immediate effect and impression if a caterer goes to visit a client to discuss a future event and takes along a small sample of goodies instead of glossy pictures and price lists. Timing of this type of presentation is obviously important; 11.45 in the morning was the time I chose for one such sales pitch: the canapés were wolfed down and then the drinks were produced and the business was secure.

If a take-away service is going to be treated seriously, an extra phone line might be necessary for orders. There should be at least two lines anyway to ensure that one is always free for incoming calls.

If catering and the take-away business increase there may be a need for additional staff, more refrigeration, and some speciality rack storage system, plus space to store new equipment and packaging materials.

Before any major expenditure is considered, realise that the kitchen is always there, day and night, and can be used, for example, at three in the morning for certain types of preparation. Split shifts and night shifts using the same number of staff cuts down heavier labour costs. Storage of certain items can be done away from the premises.

Take-away business does not necessarily mean that garish signs in neon have to flash off and on outside the door to attract the homeless and hungry at pub closing time. There are several ways of promoting take-away food which are stylish and can produce interest in buying more. Hygienic packaging must be used, reflecting the care taken in the preparation area, and detailed instructions may be needed for reheating and serving certain dishes.

Another form of the take-away business is supplying other businesses with a particular speciality off the menu, terrines and pâtés for example, or apple pie; whatever special talents emerge during the opening months: some particularly fine dishes may spring from the hands of an eager trainee who shows a certain knack and ease with something many others would find difficult.

Developing specialities and then marketing them serves the establishment well and achieves a reputation for food quality. Something like this may happen by accident. In one of my restaurants, serving individual home-made Christmas puddings to restaurant guests throughout the month of December brought large orders for the bigger version, encouraged by some printed material and tastings of different and unusual brandies and ports supplied and sponsored by the local off licence.

Other opportunities can arise on a local level. Providing a facility at a local event such as a summer fete or horse show, and by producing the appropriate style of food, whether it be barbecue or sandwiches, can bring the name of the restaurant to the public. You can have some fun as well as making a considerable profit at busy events.

When tackling any expansion of the business, ensure there is some experience in the new direction. For the novice caterer, working for a large catering company will give a good idea of the sort of organisation required to handle a large event: the essentials of booking the right amount of staff, supplying a sufficient quantity of food to cover emergencies, and how to use the left-overs; the timing of preparation and service and the estimation of how much work is entailed; how to instruct a crew, plan the evening, and keep the guests happy. All these catering skills are learned best by observing established outfits at work.

Vigilance is essential in any catering event. Food and drink on a large scale without supervision are a great temptation to temporary staff and the only effective way to control this is to have reliable management on hand throughout the event until the last bottle is counted, the van is loaded, and everyone departs into the night.

Beware of the big bag brigade in temporary staff. For large parties, experienced caterers have a system for counting alcohol with the host at the beginning, agreeing the totals with a signature from both parties to confirm them. At the end of the event, with all the bottles counted and stored in boxes, another count is done and again signatures verify the net consumption. This may be a laborious task, especially late at night after a long party; the host may say not to bother, but the next week when the bill arrives he may have changed his attitude. Some form of control must be used and agreed upon by everyone involved.

Some form of protection is also needed for the caterer in case of a delinquent client: the extravagant party for a hundred, with the caterer supplying everything from tables to flowers, champagne, food and staff, means a terrific bill. The house may look large and impressive but in reality it is rented to a tenant who will be off the next week to do a repeat performance somewhere else. An event like this needs more than a token deposit even if the client is known. Some companies are notorious for holding on to their cash, so develop a good relationship with whoever has the power to sign the cheque.

CHAPTER TEN

WHY RESTAURANTS SUCCEED OR FAIL

Restaurants succeed through the energy of their owners. The right concept in its proper setting will only work if the staff are chosen well, motivated and trained, and where the owners inspire loyalty, humour, and a constant approach. The honest, ambitious entrepreneur will strive to appreciate staff and their individual qualities, while maintaining a firm belief in providing quality at every level of operation. Success depends on the public sharing this vision of the owner's, and wanting to come back for more.

Restaurants fail when disciplines break down and there is no commitment to either product or personnel. They fail when the product is wrongly chosen and poorly located. Owners who do not allow for the lean periods and over-forecast run out of money just at the time when the business might take off.

The necessity of operating capital underlies any chance of success. First-time operations fail with inexperience at the helm and professional staff who can too easily take advantage of such a situation. And restaurants fail when the owner, often the sole proprietor, underestimates the amount of work and time which has to be contributed and does not possess the necessary strengths of discipline and sobriety. The sheer grind, and wear and tear of the nerve endings is enough to drive any decent soul to drink.

In any restaurant, there are days when disaster strikes at every turn. Coping with crises and mishaps, with staff who do not show and customers who do in droves creates tremendous pressure.

I remember one such day at Woods. We had opened the previous October and business had begun well, but the bleak days of mid January in New York do not encourage passing trade and the reservation book was now alarmingly empty — except for this particular Wednesday when, for some reason, the place was booked solid.

Extra supplies were hurriedly phoned in and extra help arrived through my Brooklyn connection; a young kid from Trinidad. It was his first day in the kitchen.

For some silly reason, I had decided to put oysters on the menu as a special appetiser, six to a serving on a bed of crushed ice — a major performance, especially with only one oyster knife in the establishment and limited experience in opening them. I decided to teach my new recruit the technique; Terence John was his name. So John began to attack these crusted creatures, but was so careful that his rate of production was scarcely one a minute. And I did not have time to do them as there was too much other preparation to get through.

By now the dining room was beginning to fill and the first orders came in. Then three heavies from Con Edison, the New York electric company, appeared, one brandishing a huge pair of wire cutters. The bill had been paid too late and no amount of begging or bribery was going to change their minds. They sauntered past five tables full of diners and turned off the power, then came back to the bar and ordered three Budweisers.

So now the power was off, we had three electricians guzzling lager at the bar, and Mrs Rockefeller arrived, gingerly picking her way down the stairs to meet her guest for lunch. The Rockefeller family owns that little bank called Chase Manhattan, and one of their branches was next door to us with a garden in between. We had our eyes on that garden for expansion.

Mrs R owned the branch and we knew we would need

her approval of the project. The branch manager was her guest.

The place was a combination of gloom lit with panic as the light outside was fading, the bartender hurried to light candles and the waiters scurried about and spilt wax as they tried to carry lit candles to each table.

Mrs R got to her table: they ordered champagne and oysters. For a main course. A dozen each. No starter. I read the check and wilted. I had eight checks on the board already and five of them included oysters.

In the dining room there was hilarity. Candles flickered at one o'clock in the afternoon and we decided to give everyone a drink on the house to buy a bit of time. The door kept opening and more people flowed in. We were full and had people waiting.

And Mrs R still had not got her oysters. Neither had tables three, seven or eleven. In the kitchen there was a minor scrum around John and his crate of oysters. And I was in sublime panic trying to complete at least one order. At last the Rockefeller order was almost ready. But just as the final oyster succumbed, Mrs R grabbed her bag, and her manager, and walked out.

The garden is still there, unkempt. The lights only came on after the fifth round of lagers and a phone call to someone who was probably imaginary.

Successful owners possess discipline and use structures to assist in dealing with so many elements and people at the same time in a limited space. Temperamental conditions have to be treated calmly, ignoring the drama of the moment. It helps to have regular routines and an interest in something entirely disconnected with the food and drink business. Yoga has calmed many a chef. Finding an empty golf course for relaxation can be difficult, but the owner should have some other interest, if only for conversation with customers when a diversion is needed.

Stress, combined with an over-indulgence in the

restaurant's products, has led to many physical failures in the industry. Avoiding stress in the first place will help to allay the overindulgences, and conscious relaxation for a fixed period daily can be of far more benefit than sprawling across three chairs and taking a boozy forty winks.

Stimulants of all types, legal and otherwise, are found in restaurants and bars and, to avoid situations which can bring reviews in the *Police Gazette* rather than *Vogue*, identify the culprits and remove them. If the owner encourages such behaviour, the artificiality of the energy behind the whole operation can be sensed in the dining room and the illusion simply fades. Bad habits breed worse ones.

The successful operators that I have met or worked with have all possessed similar qualities: attention to detail, a recognition that discipline and creativity must flourish together, and a good business sense. They have also understood the need for showmanship and they have hired accordingly.

Only by monitoring the quality and presentation of food will standards be maintained, tasting, testing and not being satisfied with second-best efforts. Chefs must accept the owner's insistence on quality, and be prepared for criticism which is constructive and not an antagonistic personal slight.

Finally, there is the sense of adventure, the element of risk taking, the plunge into unknown territory armed with a set of beliefs, blind to anything but success. This is boldness, and bold behaviour makes things happen, creates a memory, and represents strong beliefs and conviction.

The restaurant way of life is one full of variety, impossible hours of work, and theatre. It can also be heartbreaking, frustrating and dangerous to health. With the high rate of failure, and especially in periods of high interest rates, the risks must be reduced to a minimum for any chance of success. Without experience, taste, and adequate finance, there is no hope for the beginner with an average idea.

Before embarking on this particular journey, think again and listen to the intuitive senses. Providing that all the conditions are met, that there is a consensus of opinion and the gut feeling is positive, then the decision is made and there is no turning back. The excitement begins and there is no time for self doubt or questioning. You become the restaurant, flowing with the momentum, so that by the time the door opens there is such enthusiasm everywhere that it becomes infectious.

The harder part comes later after the initial excitement fades, sustaining the vibrancy in spite of decreasing business, encouraging the staff and maintaining a solid pattern of work.

The rewards of hard work, creativity and structured discipline bring great satisfaction along with cash in the bank. To be known as a genial host leads to a sociable existence and a varied lifestyle.

The process of becoming a successful restaurateur is made easier when a business starts within the capacities available and grows steadily, taking advantage of the opportunities for expansion when they occur. Success happens for those who believe they deserve it and possess the talents to achieve it.

There are a thousand and one other ways of making money with less effort and less work, and achieved with less capital for starting up. Why are restaurants such a popular form of small business operations for first-timers? The answer is simple. Running a restaurant is placing a familiar domestic scene out in the market place, knowing that by providing food, drink and service, a basic need is being catered for. And it is taste which makes for success or failure in the venture.

DIRECTORY

TRADE MAGAZINES

- *Caterer & Hotelkeeper* available at local newsagents.
- *The Restaurant Magazine* free to restaurant owners and suppliers: Quantum Publishing, 29/31 Lower Coombe Street, Croydon CR9 1LX.
- *Morning Advertiser* trade paper for the Licensed Victuallers Association, 13/27 Brunswick Place, London N16DX.
- *British Hotelier & Restaurateur* by subscription from 40 Duke Street, London W1M 6HR.

ORGANISATIONS

- *English Tourist Board* Thames Tower, Blacks Road, London W6 9EL.
- *Scottish Tourist Board* 2 Ravelston Terrace, Edinburgh EH2 3BU.
- *Wales Tourist Board* Brunel House, 2 Fitzalan Road, Cardiff CS2 1UY.
- *Hotel & Catering Training Company* International House, High Street, Ealing, London W5 5DB.
- *British Hotels, Restaurants, & Caterers Association* 40 Duke Street, London W1M 6HR.
- *The Restaurateurs Association of Great Britain* 190 Queen's Gate, London SW7 5EU.
- *Hotel, Catering & Institutional Managements Association* 191 Trinity Road, London SW17 7HN.
- *Business Expansion Scheme, BES Investment Research Ltd* The BES Association, 29 Maddox Street, London W1R 9LD.

RESTAURANT BROKERS/SPECIALIST AGENTS

- *Salmon Charles* Harvey House, Harvey Road, Leytonstone, London E11.
- *Christie & Co* 50 Victoria Street, London SW1.
- *Conrad Ritblat & Co* 14 Manchester Square, London W1M 6AA.
- *Guy Simmonds* 23 Rodney Road, Cheltenham GL5 1HX.
- *Edward Symmons & Partners* 56/62 Wilton Road, London SW1 1DH.

LEGAL CHECKLIST

With more stringent legislation affecting the catering industry, there is a greater need for serious study of the legal aspects of the restaurant business. Stricter enforcement of the laws governing hygiene has given wider powers to the Environmental Health Authority, and new laws have come into effect following recent outbreaks of salmonella, listeria and even more serious forms of food poisoning.

Liquor licensing laws have been radically altered allowing restaurants to serve alcohol from 11 am to 11 pm under the previous conditions of a restaurant licence. And certain provisions under the Employment Protection Act of 1978 have been relaxed for companies with a minimum number of employees.

Inevitably, current information on legal requirements should come from your solicitor, who should be consulted from day one. It may be worthwhile engaging a specialist lawyer when thinking of applying for a full liquor licence (the on licence), or a change of use for the premises. Remember that the more work in the simpler aspects of the law that is undertaken by the owner, the more saving is made with legal bills.

There are several sources of information about restaurant law, and more of the relevant details are covered in two publications: *The Hotel & Catering Manager's Guide to the Law* PA Chandler (New Point Publishing, 1987); *Hotel & Catering Law* Bull and Hooper (Hutchinson, 1982) *See page 148* ***Suggested Reading***.

LEGAL ESSENTIALS OF A RESTAURANT

1. *Identity* Every business functions in law as a corporate identity. The choice of format whether sole proprietorship, partnership, limited company, or cooperative is reached after tax considerations and the advice of the investors and accountant.

   Sources of information: *Starting a Business* Inland Revenue IR28; information pack from Companies House, Companies Registration Office, Maindy, Cardiff CF4 3UZ.

2. *Employment legislation*
   - The Shops Act 1950 (working conditions)
   - Wages Act 1986 (wages and holidays)
   - Equal Pay Act
   - Race Relations Act 1976
   - Sex Discrimination Act 1975
   - National Insurance Contributions (see local DHSS Office)
   - Employment Protection Act 1978
   - Health & Safety at Work Act 1974
   - Liability Insurance Employers Liability (Compulsory Insurance) Act 1969

   Sources of information: HMSO, 49 High Holborn, London WC1 and regional offices; leading booksellers who stock HMSO publications; Small Firms Service at the local office of the Department of Employment.

3. *Additional legislation*
   - Fire precautions/certificates: local Fire Officer
   - Building regulations: local Planning Office
   - Environmental health regulations: local Environmental Health Office
   - Liquor licensing (Licensing Act 1989): local justices/magistrates court (brewster sessions)
   - Liquor measurements and price display: Trading Standards Office
   - Entertainment: Performing Rights Society, 29/33 Berners Street, London W1V 1LB
   - VAT: *The VAT Guide* HM Customs & Excise (local office)

SUGGESTED READING

Accounting in the Hotel and Catering Industry R Kotas (International Text Book, 1972).

Catering Costs and Control G Paige (Cassell, 1982).

Bookkeeping and Accounts for Hotel and Catering Studies G & J Paige (Cassell, 1983).

Restaurants, Clubs and Bars F Lawson (Butterworths, 1987).

Practical Maintenance for Hoteliers, Licensees and Caterers D Gladwell (Barrie, 1974).

The White Paper on Food Safety: *Protecting the Consumer* (HMSO, 1989).

Hygiene for Management Richard Sprenger (Highfield Publications, 1989).

Legal Aspects of the Hotel & Catering Industry Richard & Stewart (Bell & Hyman, 1974).

Business Law N Savage (Butterworths, 1987).

Business Growth and *The Small Business*, leaflets available free from Department of Employment and Trade Enterprise Councils.

The World Atlas of Wine Hugh Johnson (Mitchell Beazley, 1985).

Dictionary of Wines and Spirits Pamela Vandyke Price (Peerage Books, 1986).

Christie's Wine Companion edited by Pamela Vandyke Price (Webb & Bower, 1989).

The Vegetable Book Jane Grigson (Michael Joseph, 1978; reprinted Penguin, 1988).

The Fruit Book Jane Grigson (Michael Joseph, 1982; reprinted Penguin, 1988).

English Food Jane Grigson (Macmillan, 1979; reprinted Penguin, 1987).

Secrets of the Great French Restaurants Louisette Bertholle (Papermac, 1982).

Recipes from Le Manoir aux Quat' Saisons Raymond Blanc (Macdonald/Orbis, 1988).

Leith's Cookery Course (Macdonald, 1985).

The Cook's Handbook Prue Leith (Papermac, 1986).

British Food Finds Henrietta Green (Rich & Green Ltd).

The Art of Eating M F K Fisher (Pan, 1983).

Managing for Results P Drucker (Pan, 1967).

Specialist publications from the Hotel And Catering Training Company and the regional tourist boards. *See page 145* ***Directory***.

RESTAURANT GUIDES

Just a Bite
(Egon Ronay Organisation Ltd):
tearooms, snack bars, cafes & wine bars.

AA Hotels & Restaurants in Britain
(Automobile Association).

Egon Ronay's *Cellnet Guide — Hotels and Restaurants in Great Britain and Ireland*
(Egon Ronay Organisation Ltd).

Michelin *Great Britain and Ireland*
(Red Guides, Michelin Tyre Co Ltd).

The Good Food Guide
(Consumers Association).

Britain: Hotels and Restaurants
(British Tourist Authority).

INDEX